ITALIAN VERB DRILLS

Paola Nanni-Tate

Printed on recyclable paper

PASSPORT BOOKS
a division of *NTC Publishing Group*
Lincolnwood, Illinois USA

1996 Printing

Published by Passport Books, a division of NTC Publishing Group.
© 1994 by NTC Publishing Group, 4255 West Touhy Avenue,
Lincolnwood (Chicago), Illinois 60646-1975 U.S.A.
Manufactured in the United States of America.

5 6 7 8 9 ML 9 8 7 6 5 4 3

Table of Contents

Introduction

Italian Verb Drills has been written for students of the Italian language who wish to take the time to master the structures and the conjugations of Italian verbs by learning the rules and doing the numerous exercises outlined in this book.

Italian Verb Drills covers verb tenses from the present indicative to the past subjunctive, and each tense is preceded by rules and examples to clarify its use. An answer key is supplied for the students to check their knowledge and progress, and the Indexes of Verbs list all the verbs covered in the book.

While *Italian Verb Drills* is not intended to cover "all" Italian verbs, it lists a large number of the verbs that are commonly used.

Italian Verb Drills will also serve as an example and a guide to learn other verbs that follow similar patterns.

This book has been inspired and encouraged by my husband, Bob, and by all my students, especially the ones who have studied Italian with me for a long time. To all of them I give my thanks and I dedicate *Italian Verb Drills*.

Paola Nanni-Tate

Chapter 1

Overview of Italian Verbs

1. Verb Structure

All Italian verbs have four moods: (1) The *infinitive* expresses the action itself, with no reference to time or person. It is the form given in the dictionary. (2) The *indicative* expresses a thing as a fact, and it is the most commonly used mood. It has several tenses. (3) The *imperative* is used to give orders. It has one tense (present), and it is in the 2nd person (you) with singular and plural forms, and familiar and polite forms. The 1st person plural such as *andiamo* (let's go), *mangiamo* (let's eat) is also considered imperative. (4) The *subjunctive* expresses *possibility, hopes, feelings, wishes,* and it is almost always preceded by *che,* such as in *che io venga* (that I come).

Italian verbs have two numbers: singular and plural. They have three persons.

	Singular			Plural		
1st person	*io*	*mangio*	I eat	*noi*	*mangiamo*	we eat
2nd person	*tu*	*mangi*	you eat	*voi*	*mangiate*	you eat
3rd person	*lui, lei*	*mangia*	he, she eats	*loro*	*mangiano*	they eat

2. Subject Pronouns (Pronomi Personali)

In English, the subject pronouns are always used: *I, you, he, she, it, we, you, they.* In Italian, as a general rule, they are seldom needed since the endings of the verbs give the information about the person doing the action. Only in the 3rd person singular and the 3rd person plural could there be some confusion, so it is advisable to use *lui* (he), *lei* (she), *loro* (they). *It* can be translated with *esso* or *essa,* but nowadays these forms are not very commonly used.

In Italian, there are several ways to say **you**: In the singular, there are the informal *tu* and the formal *Lei,* which is used for both men and women and which is followed by the 3rd person singular of the verb. In the plural, *Loro* and the 3rd person plural of the verb are used when talking to more than one person formally and informally. *Voi* may also be used.

Examples:	Do you speak English?
Singular:	
Informal	(Tu) parli inglese?
Formal	(Lei) parla inglese?
Plural:	
Informal	(Voi) parlate inglese?
Formal	(Loro) parlano inglese?

3. Interrogative in Italian

Usually, there is no change in the word order in Italian when asking a question, only a change of intonation when speaking, and a question mark when writing. The ***do, does, did*** in English are not translated.

    Example: Do you (informal) remember?   (Tu) ricordi?

4. Negative in Italian

The negative in Italian is formed by putting ***non*** in front of the verb. In compound tenses, ***non*** is placed in front of the auxiliary verb.

    Examples: ***Non mangio*** *niente.*   I don't eat anything.
                    Non abbiamo parlato *con lui.*   We didn't speak with him.

5. Infinitive and the Three Conjugations

All Italian verbs end in ***-are, -ere,*** or ***-ire*** in their infinitives.

    Verbs ending in ***-are*** (***mangiare,*** to eat) are in the ***1st conjugation.***
    Verbs ending in ***-ere*** (***vedere,*** to see) are in the ***2nd conjugation.***
    Verbs ending in ***-ire*** (***sentire,*** to hear) are in the ***3rd conjugation.***

Verbs Ending in *-are*

6. Present Tense of *-are* Verbs

The ***present indicative*** of regular verbs in the 1st conjugation (*-are* verbs) is formed by adding ***o, i, a, iamo, ate, ano*** to the root of the verb. The root is obtained by dropping the *-are* ending from the infinitive.

Parlare   **Mangiare**

Singular:

io parl*o*	I speak	io mangi*o*	I eat
tu parl*i*	you speak	tu mang*i*	you eat
lui parl*a*	he speaks	lui mangi*a*	he eats
lei parl*a*	she speaks	lei mangi*a*	she eats

Plural:

noi parl*iamo*	we speak	noi mang*iamo*	we eat
voi parl*ate*	you speak	voi mangi*ate*	you eat
loro parl*ano*	they speak	loro mangi*ano*	they eat

Note: *Lei parla, lei mangia* are used for ***she speaks, she eats,*** or the formal, 2nd person singular, ***you speak, you eat.***

Most verbs in the 1st conjugation are regular. (Some very common irregular ones are studied later in this chapter.) A few have some spelling differences.

   a. Verbs ending in *-care, -gare,* like ***cercare*** (to look for) and ***pagare*** (to pay), add ***h*** before endings with ***i*** or ***e*** to maintain the same sound of the root of the verb.

   Examples: ***cerco*** (I look for), ***cerchi*** (you look for).

   b. Verbs ending in *-ciare, -giare,* like ***cominciare*** (to begin) and ***mangiare*** (to eat), omit ***i*** before endings with ***e*** or ***i.***

   Examples: *mangio* (I eat), *mangi* (you eat), not ***mangii.***

   c. Verbs ending in *-iare* omit the ***i*** ending of the 2nd person singular of the present tense if the ***i*** is not in the accented syllable.

   Examples: For ***studiare*** (to study), forms are ***studio, studi,*** and not ***studii.*** For ***avviare*** (start) forms are ***avvio, avvii,*** and not ***avvi!***

7. List of Common -are Verbs

Here are some common regular verbs ending in *-are*.

abitare	to live	**litigare**	to quarrel
aiutare	to help	**mandare**	to send
arrivare	to arrive	**mostrare**	to show
ascoltare	to listen	**notare**	to notice
aspettare	to wait	**nuotare**	to swim
ballare	to dance	**pagare**	to pay
cambiare	to change	**pensare**	to think
camminare	to walk	**portare**	to bring
cantare	to sing	**pranzare**	to have lunch
cenare	to have supper	**provare**	to try
cominciare	to start	**raccontare**	to narrate
contare	to count	**rallentare**	to slow down
dimenticare	to forget	**regalare**	to give a gift
domandare	to ask	**ricordare**	to remember
fermare	to stop, to close	**riposare**	to rest
giocare	to play	**ritornare**	to return
girare	to turn	**saltare**	to jump
guidare	to drive	**spiegare**	to explain
gustare	to taste	**studiare**	to study
imparare	to learn	**suonare**	to play
insegnare	to teach	**tagliare**	to cut
lasciare	to leave, to let	**trovare**	to find
lavare	to wash	**viaggiare**	to travel
lavorare	to work	**volare**	to fly

8. Practice

Note: All regular verbs ending in *-are* form the present indicative like the models in part 6. Write the *present tense* of the verbs.

1. **cantare**   io _____   tu _____   lui, lei _____

   (to sing)   noi _____   voi _____   loro _____

2. **provare**   io _____   tu _____   lui, lei _____

   (to try)   noi _____   voi _____   loro _____

3. **lavorare**   io _____   tu _____   lui, lei _____

   (to work)   noi _____   voi _____   loro _____

4. **ricordare**   io _____   tu _____   lui, lei _____

   (to remember)   noi _____   voi _____   loro _____

5. **viaggiare**   io _____   tu _____   lui, lei _____

   (to travel)   noi _____   voi _____   loro _____

6. **volare**   io _____   tu _____   lui, lei _____

   (to fly)   noi _____   voi _____   loro _____

9. Practice

Write the *present tense* of the verbs in the person indicated by the pronoun.

Io:

studiare	insegnare	viaggiare	saltare
_____	_____	_____	_____

Tu:

parlare	mangiare	trovare	ballare
_____	_____	_____	_____

Lui, Lei:

imparare	entrare	lavare	riposare
_____	_____	_____	_____

Noi:

comprare	arrivare	aiutare	tagliare
_____	_____	_____	_____

Voi:

parlare	imparare	aspettare	pensare
_____	_____	_____	_____

Loro:

spiegare	insegnare	contare	camminare
_____	_____	_____	_____

10. Practice

Write the *present tense* of the verb in the person indicated by the pronoun.

1. Noi (mangiare) _____

2. Lui (imparare) _____

3. Loro (comprare) _____

4. Io (cantare) _____

5. Tu (camminare) _____

6. Voi (parlare) _____

7. Noi (studiare) _____

8. Lei (cambiare) _____

9. Voi (pensare) _____

10. Lei (nuotare) _____

11. Io (giocare) _____

12. Noi (pranzare) _____

13. Voi (viaggiare) _____

14. Loro (ballare) _____

15. Lei (lavorare) _____

16. Noi (lavare) _____

17. Io (pensare) _____

18. Noi (imparare) _____

19. Io (ascoltare) _____

20. Lei (amare) _____

21. Voi (abitare) _____

22. Loro (pagare) _____

23. Tu (entrare) _____

24. Noi (ispezionare) _____

25. Lui (pensare) _____

26. Tu (mandare) _____

11. Practice

Rewrite in English in the right form and person.

1. Mangiamo _____

2. Imparo _____

3. Comprano _____

4. Canto _____

5. Cammini _____

6. Parlate _____

7. Studiamo _____

8. Cambio _____

9. Pensate _____

10. Nuoto _____

11. Gioco _____

12. Pranziamo _____

13. Viaggiate _____

14. Ballano _____

15. Lavora _____

16. Laviamo _____

17. Penso _____

18. Impariamo _____

19. Ascolto _____

20. Ama _____

21. Abitate _____

22. Pagano _____

23. Entri _____

24. Ispezioniamo _____

25. Pensa _____

26. Mandi _____

12. Practice

Rewrite in Italian.

1. I eat_____
2. You (s.) think_____
3. They learn_____
4. We sing_____
5. You (pl.) eat_____
6. He studies_____
7. She teaches_____
8. I learn_____
9. You (s.) work_____
10. They wash_____
11. She enters_____
12. We rest_____

13. You (s.) wait_____
14. They sing_____
15. I dance_____
16. We jump_____
17. I travel_____
18. He finds_____
19. We arrive_____
20. You (pl.) wait_____
21. She helps_____
22. I buy_____
23. She finds_____
24. We study_____

Negative and Interrogative Forms

Rewrite in Italian.

1. I don't eat_____
2. You (s.) don't work_____
3. We don't remember_____
4. They don't work_____
5. She doesn't enter_____
6. I don't rest_____

7. Do you (s.) eat? _____
8. Do you (s.) work? _____
9. Do we remember? _____
10. Do they work? _____
11. Does she enter? _____
12. Do I rest? _____

13. Practice

Rewrite in English.

1. Parliamo _____

2. Salti _____

3. Pensa _____

4. Cantate _____

5. Suono _____

6. Mangiamo _____

7. Imparano _____

8. Trovi _____

9. Entriamo _____

10. Lavori _____

11. Insegniamo _____

12. Lavate _____

13. Riposo _____

14. Guarda _____

15. Camminiamo _____

16. Portate _____

17. Balli _____

18. Parlano _____

19. Viaggia _____

20. Aiutiamo _____

21. Ricordo _____

22. Dimentica _____

23. Non mangio _____

24. Non camminano _____

25. Non lavorate _____

26. Lavori? _____

14. Irregular Verbs Ending in -are

In the 1st conjugation, there are four irregular verbs:

stare	to stay	*fare*	to make, to do
dare	to give	*andare*	to go

The following are the conjugation of these irregular verbs:

Stare

io	*sto*	I stay
tu	*stai*	you stay
lui	*sta*	he stays
lei	*sta*	she stays
noi	*stiamo*	we stay
voi	*state*	you stay
loro	*stanno*	they stay

Dare

io	*do*	I give
tu	*dai*	you give
lui	*dà*	he gives
lei	*dà*	she gives
noi	*diamo*	we give
voi	*date*	you give
loro	*danno*	they give

Fare

io	*faccio*	I make, I do
tu	*fai*	you make, you do
lui	*fa*	he makes, he does
lei	*fa*	she makes, she does
noi	*facciamo*	we make, we do
voi	*fate*	you make, you do
loro	*fanno*	they make, they do

Andare

io	*vado*	I go
tu	*vai*	you go
lui	*va*	he goes
lei	*va*	she goes
noi	*andiamo*	we go
voi	*andate*	you go
loro	*vanno*	they go

15. Practice

Write the *present tense* of the verbs.

1. **dare**   io _____   tu _____   lui, lei _____

   (to give)   noi _____   voi _____   loro _____

2. **fare**   io _____   tu _____   lui, lei _____

   (to make, do) noi _____   voi _____   loro _____

3. **stare**   io _____   tu _____   lui, lei _____

   (to stay)   noi _____   voi _____   loro _____

4. **andare**   io _____   tu _____   lui, lei _____

   (to go)   noi _____   voi _____   loro _____

Chapter 2

Verbs Ending in -ere

1. Present Tense of -ere Verbs

All the verbs ending in **-ere,** such as **temere** (to fear), belong to the 2nd conjugation. The **present** indicative of verbs in the 2nd conjugation is formed by adding **o, i, e, iamo, ete, ono** to the root of the verb.

Vedere		To see		**Scrivere**		To write
io	ved*o*	I see		io	scriv*o*	I write
tu	ved*i*	you see		tu	scriv*i*	you write
lui	ved*e*	he sees		lui	scriv*e*	he writes
lei	ved*e*	she sees		lei	scriv*e*	she writes
noi	ved*iamo*	we see		noi	scriv*iamo*	we write
voi	ved*ete*	you see		voi	scriv*ete*	you write
loro	ved*ono*	they see		loro	scriv*ono*	they write

In the present tense of some **-ere** verbs, the pronunciation changes, but the spelling of the root and the endings stay the same. In verbs ending in **-cere** and **-gere,** such as **vincere** (to win) and **leggere** (to read), the pronunciation changes to a hard sound when the **o** or **a** follows **c** or **g.**

Examples: Vin*co,* vinci, vince, vinciamo, vincete, vin*cono*
Leg*go,* leggi, legge, leggiamo, leggete, legg*ono*

2. List of Common *-ere* Verbs

Here are some common verbs ending in *-ere.*

accadere	to happen	**esistere**	to exist
accedere	to access	**godere**	to enjoy
accendere	to turn on	**includere**	to include
apprendere	to learn	**insistere**	to insist
assistere	to assist	**leggere**	to read
assolvere	to absolve	**mettere**	to put
assumere	to assume, hire	**nascondere**	to hide
attendere	to wait for, attend	**perdere**	to lose
cadere	to fall	**permettere**	to allow
cedere	to yield	**piangere**	to cry
chiedere	to ask	**prendere**	to take
chiudere	to close	**pretendere**	to pretend
comprendere	to comprehend	**promettere**	to promise
concludere	to conclude	**promuovere**	to promote
condividere	to share	**ridere**	to laugh
confondere	to confuse	**risolvere**	to resolve
conoscere	to know	**rispondere**	to answer
consistere	to consist	**rompere**	to break
convincere	to convince	**scendere**	to descend
correggere	to correct	**scrivere**	to write
correre	to run	**sorridere**	to smile
credere	to believe	**spingere**	to push
crescere	to grow	**succedere**	to happen
decidere	to decide	**temere**	to fear
difendere	to defend	**trasmettere**	to broadcast
discutere	to discuss	**vedere**	to see
distinguere	to distinguish	**vincere**	to win
dividere	to divide	**vivere**	to live

Note: Some of the above verbs are irregular in other forms, but they all form the *present indicative* with the regular endings.

3. Practice

Note: Most verbs in *-ere* form the present tense like the above models in part 1.
Write the *present tense* of the verbs.

1. **dividere**   io _____   tu _____   lui, lei _____

   (to divide)   noi _____   voi _____   loro_____

2. **chiudere**   io _____   tu _____   lui, lei _____

   (to close)   noi _____   voi _____   loro_____

3. **mettere**   io _____   tu _____   lui, lei _____

   (to put)   noi _____   voi _____   loro_____

4. **convincere**   io _____   tu _____   lui, lei _____

   (to convince)   noi _____   voi _____   loro_____

5. **spingere**   io _____   tu _____   lui, lei _____

   (to push)   noi _____   voi _____   loro_____

6. **perdere**   io _____   tu _____   lui, lei _____

   (to lose)   noi _____   voi _____   loro_____

4. Practice

Write the present tense of the verbs in the person indicated.

Io:

apprendere	attendere	chiedere	chiudere
_____	_____	_____	_____

Tu:

cadere	confondere	dividere	crescere
_____	_____	_____	_____

Lui, Lei:

decidere	difendere	discutere	concludere
_____	_____	_____	_____

Noi:

apprendere	attendere	insistere	esistere
_____	_____	_____	_____

Voi:

cadere	ridere	rispondere	nascondere
_____	_____	_____	_____

Loro:

perdere	piangere	insistere	promettere
_____	_____	_____	_____

5. Practice

Rewrite in Italian.

1. I fear _____

2. You (s.) wait for _____

3. He falls _____

4. We ask _____

5. You (s.) assist _____

6. He closes _____

7. They confuse _____

8. You (s.) know _____

9. They decide _____

10. He defends _____

11. She discusses _____

12. We decide_____

13. He asks _____

14. You (s.) enjoy _____

15. I conclude_____

16. She insists_____

17. We put _____

18. He loses _____

19. I promise _____

20. We promise _____

21. We cry _____

22. They answer_____

23. I see _____

24. She sees _____

25. I write_____

26. I cry _____

Negative and Interrogative Forms

Rewrite in Italian.

1. I don't assist_____

2. You don't (s.) wait for _____

3. We don't ask _____

4. They don't divide_____

5. She doesn't close _____

6. He doesn't cry _____

7. Do you (s.) assist? _____

8. Do you (s.) wait for?_____

9. Do you (s.) ask?_____

10. Do they divide? _____

11. Do you (s.) close? _____

12. Do you (s.) cry?_____

6. Practice

Rewrite in English.

1. Apprendiamo _____
2. Teme _____
3. Assumiamo _____
4. Attendono _____
5. Cado _____
6. Credete _____
7. Chiede _____
8. Chiudono _____
9. Correggi _____
10. Concludete _____
11. Condividono _____
12. Confondono _____
13. Conosci _____
14. Conoscono _____
15. Cuocete _____
16. Cuoce _____
17. Decido _____
18. Difendete _____
19. Discutiamo _____
20. Includiamo _____
21. Insiste _____
22. Perdete _____
23. Perdono _____
24. Piangono _____
25. Pretende _____
26. Rispondi _____
27. Vedo _____
28. Vinci _____
29. Conosce _____
30. Vincono _____
31. Ridete _____
32. Rompono _____
33. Non rimango _____
34. Non permettono _____
35. Non leggiamo _____
36. Leggete? _____
37. Leggi? _____
38. Vediamo? _____
39. Scrive? _____
40. Temono? _____
41. Non vedete? _____
42. Non leggi? _____
43. Non scrivono? _____
44. Non scriviamo? _____

7. Irregular Verbs Ending in *-ere*

In the 2nd conjugation, there are many irregular verbs. Here are some of the most common.

Bere		To drink	**Cogliere**		To gather
io	*bevo*	I drink	*io*	*colgo*	I gather
tu	*bevi*	you drink	*tu*	*cogli*	you gather
lui	*beve*	he drinks	*lui*	*coglie*	he gathers
lei	*beve*	she drinks	*lei*	*coglie*	she gathers
noi	*beviamo*	we drink	*noi*	*cogliamo*	we gather
voi	*bevete*	you drink	*voi*	*cogliete*	you gather
loro	*bevono*	they drink	*loro*	*colgono*	they gather

Dovere		Must, to have to	**Porre**		To put
io	*devo*	I must/have to	*io*	*pongo*	I put
tu	*devi*	you must/have to	*tu*	*poni*	you put
lui	*deve*	he must/has to	*lui*	*pone*	he puts
lei	*deve*	she must/has to	*lei*	*pone*	she puts
noi	*dobbiamo*	we must/have to	*noi*	*poniamo*	we put
voi	*dovete*	you must/have to	*voi*	*ponete*	you put
loro	*devono*	they must/have to	*loro*	*pongono*	they put

Potere		To be able	**Rimanere**		To stay
io	*posso*	I am able	*io*	*rimango*	I stay
tu	*puoi*	you are able	*tu*	*rimani*	you stay
lui	*può*	he is able	*lui*	*rimane*	he stays
lei	*può*	she is able	*lei*	*rimane*	she stays
noi	*possiamo*	we are able	*noi*	*rimaniamo*	we stay
voi	*potete*	you are able	*voi*	*rimanete*	you stay
loro	*possono*	they are able	*loro*	*rimangono*	they stay

Sapere		To know	**Scegliere**		To choose
io	*so*	I know	*io*	*scelgo*	I choose
tu	*sai*	you know	*tu*	*scegli*	you choose
lui	*sa*	he knows	*lui*	*sceglie*	he chooses
lei	*sa*	she knows	*lei*	*sceglie*	she chooses
noi	*sappiamo*	we know	*noi*	*scegliamo*	we choose
voi	*sapete*	you know	*voi*	*scegliete*	you choose
loro	*sanno*	they know	*loro*	*scelgono*	they choose

Sedere		To sit	**Spegnere**		To turn off
io	*siedo*	I sit	*io*	*spengo*	I turn off
tu	*siedi*	you sit	*tu*	*spegni*	you turn off
lui	*siede*	he sits	*lui*	*spegne*	he turns off
lei	*siede*	she sits	*lei*	*spegne*	she turns off
noi	*sediamo*	we sit	*noi*	*spegniamo*	we turn off
voi	*sedete*	you sit	*voi*	*spegnete*	you turn off
loro	*siedono*	they sit	*loro*	*spengono*	they turn off

Tenere	To keep	**Volere**	To want
io tengo	I keep	*io voglio*	I want
tu tieni	you keep	*tu vuoi*	you want
lui tiene	he keeps	*lui vuole*	he wants
lei tiene	she keeps	*lei vuole*	she wants
noi teniamo	we keep	*noi vogliamo*	we want
voi tenete	you keep	*voi volete*	you want
loro tengono	they keep	*loro vogliono*	they want

8. Practice

Write the *present tense* of the verbs.

1. **dovere**   io _____   tu _____   lui, lei _____

   (must)   noi _____   voi _____   loro _____

2. **scegliere**   io _____   tu _____   lui, lei _____

   (to choose)   noi _____   voi _____   loro _____

3. **potere**   io _____   tu _____   lui, lei _____

   (to be able)   noi _____   voi _____   loro _____

4. **sapere**   io _____   tu _____   lui, lei _____

   (to know)   noi _____   voi _____   loro _____

5. **tenere**   io _____   tu _____   lui, lei _____

   (to keep)   noi _____   voi _____   loro _____

6. **volere**   io _____   tu _____   lui, lei _____

   (to want)   noi _____   voi _____   loro _____

Verbs Ending in *-ire*

9. Present Indicative of *-ire* Verbs

All the verbs ending in *ire,* such as *partire* (to depart, to leave) and *dormire* (to sleep), belong to the 3rd conjugation.

The *present indicative* of verbs in the 3rd conjugation is formed by adding *o, i, e, iamo, ite, ono* to the root of the verb. Many verbs of the 3rd conjugation insert *isc* between the root and the endings of the present tense.

Dormire		To sleep	**Finire**		To finish
io	dorm*o*	I sleep	io	fin*isco*	I finish
tu	dorm*i*	you sleep	tu	fin*isci*	you finish
lui	dorm*e*	he sleeps	lui	fin*isce*	he finishes
lei	dorm*e*	she sleeps	lei	fin*isce*	she finishes
noi	dorm*iamo*	we sleep	noi	fin*iamo*	we finish
voi	dorm*ite*	you sleep	voi	fin*ite*	you finish
loro	dorm*ono*	they sleep	loro	fin*iscono*	they finish

The following *-ire* verbs do not insert *isc* when conjugated:

acconsentire	to agree	**fuggire**	to escape
applaudire	to applaud	**inghiottire**	to swallow
aprire	to open	**inseguire**	to follow
assentire	to agree, to consent	**investire**	to invest
avvertire	to announce	**mentire**	to lie
bollire	to boil	**offrire**	to offer
conseguire	to result	**partire**	to leave, depart
consentire	to agree	**seguire**	to follow
convertire	to convert	**sentire**	to hear
coprire	to cover	**servire**	to serve
divertire	to enjoy	**soffrire**	to suffer
eseguire	to do	**vestire**	to dress

The following *-ire* verbs insert *isc* in the present tense of the indicative.

aderire	to adhere	**guarire**	to heal
attribuire	to attribute	**impazzire**	to go mad
benedire	to bless	**inserire**	to insert
capire	to understand	**istruire**	to instruct
colpire	to hit	**preferire**	to prefer
costruire	to build	**pulire**	to clean
definire	to define	**punire**	to punish
digerire	to digest	**restituire**	to return
dimagrire	to lose weight	**riunire**	to meet
esaurire	to exhaust	**sostituire**	to substitute
esibire	to exhibit	**spedire**	to send
fallire	to fail	**stabilire**	to establish
ferire	to wound	**suggerire**	to suggest
finire	to finish	**tradire**	to betray
garantire	to guarantee	**trasferire**	to transfer
gestire	to manage	**ubbidire**	to obey

Note: Some of the above verbs are irregular, but they all form the present indicative with regular endings.

10. Practice

Most verbs ending in *-ire* form the present indicative like the models on page 21.
Write the *present tense* of the verbs.

1. **avvertire**   io _____   tu _____   lui, lei _____

   (to notify)   noi _____   voi _____   loro _____

2. **bollire**   io _____   tu _____   lui, lei _____

   (to boil)   noi _____   voi _____   loro _____

3. **sentire**   io _____   tu _____   lui, lei _____

   (to hear)   noi _____   voi _____   loro _____

4. **capire**   io _____   tu _____   lui, lei _____

   (to understand)   noi _____   voi _____   loro _____

5. **preferire**   io _____   tu _____   lui, lei _____

   (to prefer)   noi _____   voi _____   loro _____

11. Practice

Write the *present tense* of the following *-ire* verbs in the indicated person.

Io:

aprire	capire	offrire	finire
_____	_____	_____	_____

Tu:

dormire	avvertire	bollire	sentire
_____	_____	_____	_____

Lui, Lei:

preferire	partire	vestire	spedire
_____	_____	_____	_____

Noi:

servire	vestire	aprire	capire
_____	_____	_____	_____

Voi:

avvertire	seguire	costruire	istruire
_____	_____	_____	_____

Loro:

sentire	inseguire	investire	partire
_____	_____	_____	_____

12. Practice

Rewrite in Italian.

1. I prefer _____
2. You (s.) consent _____
3. He covers _____
4. We enjoy _____
5. They escape _____
6. He understands _____
7. He follows _____
8. You (s.) lie _____
9. I hear _____
10. We suffer _____
11. They open _____
12. He finishes _____

13. You (s.) applaud _____
14. He converts _____
15. I applaud _____
16. He sleeps _____
17. I swallow _____
18. You (pl.) leave _____
19. They serve _____
20. I sleep _____
21. She prefers _____
22. I understand _____
23. We prefer _____
24. I build _____

Negative and Interrogative Forms

Rewrite in Italian.

1. I don't finish _____
2. He doesn't understand _____
3. They don't instruct _____
4. You (s.) don't hear _____
5. I don't sleep _____
6. We don't applaud _____
7. We don't leave _____
8. I don't suffer _____

9. Do we build? _____
10. Does he hear? _____
11. Do they understand? _____
12. Do they hear? _____
13. Does he sleep? _____
14. Do you consent? _____
15. Does she finish? _____
16. Do we depart? _____

13. Practice

Rewrite in English.

1. Acconsenti_____
2. Applaudono_____
3. Apre_____
4. Aprono_____
5. Avvertiamo_____
6. Bolle _____
7. Capisco _____
8. Consentite _____
9. Convertono _____
10. Copro_____
11. Costruisce _____
12. Offre _____
13. Divertiamo_____
14. Dormite_____
15. Seguono _____
16. Finiamo_____
17. Fugge_____

18. Guarisci_____
19. Garantiscono _____
20. Inghiotti_____
21. Inseguono _____
22. Istruisce_____
23. Preferiscono _____
24. Seguite _____
25. Pulite_____
26. Puniscono _____
27. Colpisce _____
28. Servo_____
29. Soffre _____
30. Sostituisco_____
31. Spediamo _____
32. Sostituiscono_____
33. Suggeriamo_____
34. Trasferiscono _____

Negative and Interrogative Forms

1. Non dormiamo _____
2. Non soffre_____
3. Non capiamo_____
4. Non istruisce_____
5. Non apri _____

6. Acconsenti?_____
7. Partono? _____
8. Dormi? _____
9. Capisci?_____
10. Pulite?_____

14. Irregular Verb Endings in *-ire*

In the 3rd conjugation, there are many irregular verbs. The most common are:

dire	to tell, say	*udire*	to hear
morire	to die	*uscire*	to go out, exit
salire	to go up, ascend	*venire*	to come

The following are the conjugations of the present indicative of the above verbs:

Dire		To tell, say		**Morire**		To die	
io	dico	I tell, say		io	muoio	I die	
tu	dici	you tell, say		tu	muori	you die	
lui	dice	he tells, says		lui	muore	he dies	
lei	dice	she tells, says		lei	muore	she dies	
noi	diciamo	we tell, say		noi	moriamo	we die	
voi	dite	you tell, say		voi	morite	you die	
loro	dicono	they tell, say		loro	muoiono	they die	

Salire		To climb		**Udire**		To hear	
io	salgo	I climb		io	odo	I hear	
tu	sali	you climb		tu	odi	you hear	
lui	sale	he climbs		lui	ode	he hears	
lei	sale	she climbs		lei	ode	she hears	
noi	saliamo	we climb		noi	udiamo	we hear	
voi	salite	you climb		voi	udite	you hear	
loro	salgono	they climb		loro	odono	they hear	

Uscire		To go out		**Venire**		To come	
io	esco	I go out		io	vengo	I come	
tu	esci	you go out		tu	vieni	you come	
lui	esce	he goes out		lui	viene	he comes	
lei	esce	she goes out		lei	viene	she comes	
noi	usciamo	we go out		noi	veniamo	we come	
voi	uscite	you go out		voi	venite	you come	
loro	escono	they go out		loro	vengono	they come	

15. Practice

Write the *present tense* of the verbs.

1. **venire**   io _____   tu _____   lui, lei _____

   (to come)   noi _____   voi _____   loro _____

2. **dire**   io _____   tu _____   lui, lei _____

   (to say)   noi _____   voi _____   loro _____

3. **uscire**   io _____   tu _____   lui, lei _____

   (to go out)   noi _____   voi _____   loro _____

16. Practice

Rewrite in Italian.

1. you (s.) say _____

2. they go out _____

3. we come _____

4. they die _____

5. I climb _____

6. she says _____

7. I go out _____

8. they come _____

9. they climb _____

10. we go out _____

11. you (pl.) climb _____

12. he dies _____

13. you (s.) hear _____

14. they say _____

15. we hear _____

16. you (pl.) say _____

Chapter 3

Imperative

1. Uses of the Imperative: Familiar Forms

The *imperative* is for commands and orders. It is used in the *tu* and *voi* forms, *tu* for singular, familiar and *voi* for the plural, familiar. The forms are similar to the present tense except for the *tu* form of the 1st conjugation, which ends in *a* instead of *i.*

    Examples: *parla* (speak) instead of *parli, mangia* (eat), instead of *mangi*

The 1st person plural of the present tense can be used in the imperative, but it is mostly a suggestion and an urgent request rather than a command.

    Examples: *scriviamo* (let's write), *mangiamo* (let's eat), *andiamo* (let's go)

The negative *imperative* for *tu* is formed by *non* + the infinitive of the verb.

    Example: *Non parlare* (don't speak), *non andare* (don't go)

For the 2nd person plural or *voi, non* is put in front of the *imperative* form.

    Example: *Non parlate* (don't speak), *non scrivete* (don't write)

    Note: The formal forms of the imperative are introduced on page 32.

2. Familiar Imperative Forms

parla (speak)	*scrivi* (write)	*pulisci* (clean)
parliamo (let's speak)	*scriviamo* (let's write)	*puliamo* (let's clean)
parlate (speak pl.)	*scrivete* (write pl.)	*pulite* (clean pl.)

Negative:

non parlare (don't speak)	*non scrivere* (don't write)	*non pulire* (don't clean)
non parlate (don't speak pl.)	*non scrivete* (don't write pl.)	*non pulite* (don't clean pl.)

3. Practice

Rewrite in Italian in the imperative. Use the singular form unless plural (pl.) is indicated.

1. Speak _____
2. Sing _____
3. Go (pl.) _____
4. Don't go _____
5. Let's go _____
6. Don't eat (pl.) _____
7. Let's finish _____
8. Don't play (pl.) _____
9. Play _____
10. Look _____
11. Listen _____
12. Don't leave _____
13. Let's leave _____
14. Play (pl.) _____
15. Let's play _____
16. Go out _____
17. Don't go out (pl.) _____

18. Play _____
19. Don't play _____
20. Eat (pl.) _____
21. Write _____
22. Don't write _____
23. Let's write _____
24. Close _____
25. Don't close _____
26. Let's close _____
27. Sleep _____
28. Sleep (pl.) _____
29. Drink _____
30. Drink (pl.) _____
31. Read _____
32. Let's read _____
33. Don't read _____
34. Don't read (pl.) _____

4. Practice

Rewrite in English.

1. Parlate _____
2. Canta _____
3. Non cantare _____
4. Ascolta _____
5. Ascoltate _____
6. Andiamo _____
7. Parla _____
8. Non parlare _____
9. Giochiamo _____
10. Non giocate _____
11. Uscite _____
12. Non uscire _____
13. Mangia _____
14. Mangiamo _____
15. Chiudi _____
16. Chiedete _____
17. Pensa _____
18. Non pensate _____
19. Suggerisci _____
20. Parti _____
21. Mettete _____
22. Non mettere _____
23. Spera _____
24. Entrate _____
25. Studia _____
26. Non studiare _____
27. Non partite _____
28. Canta _____
29. Cantiamo _____
30. Spingi _____
31. Non spingere _____
32. Prendete _____

5. Irregular Imperative

There are a few irregular verbs with an irregular *tu* form of the imperative. They are:

	Imperative	
andare (to go)	*và* or *vai*	
avere (to have)	*abbi*	*abbiate* (irregular plural)
dare (to give)	*dà* or *dai*	
dire (to say, to tell)	*dì*	
essere (to be)	*sii*	*siate* (irregular plural)
stare (to stay)	*stà* or *stai*	

6. The *Lei* and *Loro* Forms of the Imperative

The *imperative* for *Lei* and *Loro* is the same as the 3rd person of the present subjunctive (chapter 7). These forms are the formal polite forms.

	Parlare	*Scrivere*	*Sentire*	*Finire*
Lei	*parli*	*scriva*	*senta*	*finisca*
Loro	*parlino*	*scrivano*	*sentano*	*finiscano*

Examples:

Singular:

Parli con la signora!	Speak with the lady!
Scriva subito la lettera!	Write the letter immediately!
Senta la radio!	Listen to the radio!
Finisca di mangiare!	Finish eating!

Plural:

Parlino con la signora!	Speak with the lady!
Scrivano subito!	Write immediately!
Sentano la radio!	Listen to the radio!
Finiscano di mangiare!	Finish eating!

Many of the common verbs have irregular command forms for the polite singular and plural. Following are the most common.

	Singular	**Plural**
andare (to go)	*vada*	*vadano*
bere (to drink)	*beva*	*bevano*
dare (to give)	*dia*	*diano*
dire (to tell, say)	*dica*	*dicano*
fare (to do, to make)	*faccia*	*facciano*
stare (to stay)	*stia*	*stiano*
temere (to fear)	*tema*	*temano*
venire (to come)	*venga*	*vengano*

The *negative imperative* formal is formed by placing *non* before the affirmative.

Examples:	*Non parli!*	Don't speak!
	Non scrivano!	Don't write!

Object and reflexive pronouns *always precede* the *Lei* and *Loro* forms.

Examples:	*Mi scriva!*	Write me!
	Non mi scriva!	Don't write to me!

7. Practice

Rewrite in English, using the *polite forms* of the *imperative* singular and plural as indicated.

1. Wait (s.) _____

2. Wait (pl.)_____

3. Pay (s.) _____

4. Pay (pl.)_____

5. Eat (s.) _____

6. Answer (pl.) _____

7. Finish (s.) _____

8. Look (pl.) _____

9. Come (s.) _____

10. Eat (pl.)_____

11. Answer (s.)_____

12. Finish (pl.)_____

13. Come (pl.)_____

14. Go out (s.) _____

15. Leave (pl.)_____

16. Tell me (s.)_____

17. Think (s.) _____

18. Go out (pl.)_____

19. Walk (s.)_____

20. Sing (pl.)_____

21. Read (pl.) _____

22. Smile (s.) _____

Future

8. Forms of the Future

The *future tense* in Italian consists of a single verb while in English it consists of the auxiliary **shall** or **will** and the infinitive of the verb. The future of regular verbs is formed by putting the future endings on the infinitive of the verb without the final *e.* In the 1st conjugation, the *a* of the infinitive ending changes to *e* in the future.

Examples:	*Parlare* (to speak)	*Scrivere* (to write)	*Sentire* (to hear)
	Parlerò (I'll speak)	*Scriverò* (I'll write)	*Sentirò* (I'll hear)

Parlare		**Scrivere**		**Sentire**	
io	parler*ò*	io	scriver*ò*	io	sentir*ò*
tu	parler*ai*	tu	scriver*ai*	tu	sentir*ai*
lui	parler*à*	lui	scriver*à*	lui	sentir*à*
lei	parler*à*	lei	scriver*à*	lei	sentir*à*
noi	parler*emo*	noi	scriver*emo*	noi	sentir*emo*
voi	parler*ete*	voi	scriver*ete*	voi	sentir*ete*
loro	parler*anno*	loro	scriver*anno*	loro	sentir*anno*

Note: The 1st and the 3rd persons singular have an accent on the ending. This means that the last syllable must be stressed.

Verbs ending in *-care* and *-gare* add an *h* to the future tense stem to keep the hard *c* and *g* sounds.

Examples:	*Pagare* (to pay)	*Io pagherò* (I'll pay)
	Giocare (to play)	*Io giocherò* (I'll play)

Verbs ending in *-ciare* and *-giare* drop the *i* in the future tense stem.

Examples:	*Cominciare* (to begin)	*Io comincerò* (I'll begin)
	Mangiare (to eat)	*Io mangerò* (I'll eat)

Here are some verbs that have irregular stems in the future. The endings are the same as the regular future endings.

Infinitive	**Future Stem**	**Conjugation**
andare (to go)	*andr*	andrò, andrai, andrà, etc.
avere (to have)	*avr*	avrò, avrai, avrà, etc.
bere (to drink)	*berr*	berrò, berrai, berrà, etc.
cadere (to fall)	*cadr*	cadrò, cadrai, cadrà, etc.
dare (to give)	*dar*	darò, darai, darà, etc.
essere (to be)	*sar*	sarò, sarai, sarà, etc.
fare (to make)	*far*	farò, farai, farà, etc.
porre (to put)	*porr*	porrò, porrai, porrà, etc.
sapere (to know)	*sapr*	saprò, saprai, saprà, etc.
tenere (to hold)	*terr*	terrò, terrai, terrà, etc.
vedere (to see)	*vedr*	vedrò, vedrai, vedrà, etc.
venire (to come)	*verr*	verrò, verrai, verrà, etc.

9. Practice

Write the *future* tense of the verbs.

1. **vedere**   io _____   tu _____   lui, lei _____

    (to see)   noi _____   voi _____   loro _____

2. **andare**   io _____   tu _____   lui, lei _____

    (to go)   noi _____   voi _____   loro _____

3. **capire**   io _____   tu _____   lui, lei _____

    (to understand)   noi _____   voi _____   loro _____

4. **aiutare**   io _____   tu _____   lui, lei _____

    (to help)   noi _____   voi _____   loro _____

10. Practice

Write the verbs in the *future* tense in the person indicated.

Io:

parlare   vedere   pulire

_____   _____   _____

Tu:

viaggiare   permettere   capire

_____   _____   _____

Lui, Lei:

trovare   sapere   sentire

_____   _____   _____

Noi:

guardare   bere   finire

_____   _____   _____

Voi:

lavorare   avere   partire

_____   _____   _____

Loro:

andare   essere   sentire

_____   _____   _____

11. Practice

Rewrite in English.

1. Capirò _____
2. Lavorerò _____
3. Leggerai _____
4. Canterà _____
5. Sentirete _____
6. Pianterai _____
7. Ascolterò _____
8. Pianterete _____
9. Vedremo _____
10. Risponderanno _____
11. Pagherò _____
12. Giocheremo _____
13. Penserai _____
14. Vedrete _____
15. Sentirai _____
16. Deciderò _____
17. Piangeremo _____
18. Vincerà _____
19. Discuterete _____

20. Andremo _____
21. Studierò _____
22. Penserete _____
23. Scriverai _____
24. Cuocerò _____
25. Finirò _____
26. Giocheremo _____
27. Staremo _____
28. Farai _____
29. Darete _____
30. Partirai _____
31. Direte _____
32. Dormiremo _____
33. Inseguirai _____
34. Verremo _____
35. Bollirò _____
36. Applaudiranno _____
37. Aprirà _____
38. Saliremo _____

Negative Future Forms

Rewrite in English.

1. Non mangerò _____
2. Non andremo _____
3. Non farà _____

4. Non canteremo _____
5. Non capirà _____
6. Non finirete _____

12. Practice

Rewrite in Italian.

1. I'll attend _____
2. He'll fall _____
3. We'll write _____
4. They'll think _____
5. We'll understand _____
6. I'll close _____
7. You'll (s.) speak _____
8. We'll play _____
9. They'll travel _____
10. I'll put _____
11. We'll do _____
12. He'll find _____
13. We'll find _____
14. I'll listen _____
15. We'll learn _____
16. I'll eat _____
17. We'll go _____
18. They'll make _____
19. I'll stay _____
20. I'll buy _____
21. They'll come _____
22. I'll come _____
23. We'll look _____
24. We'll say _____
25. He'll tell _____
26. They'll sing _____
27. We'll cry _____
28. I'll plant _____
29. We'll go out _____
30. They'll climb _____
31. You'll (pl.) go _____
32. We'll follow _____
33. He'll insist _____
34. She'll see _____
35. We'll answer _____
36. I'll pay _____
37. We'll vote _____
38. I'll decide _____
39. We'll drink _____
40. We'll hear _____

Negative Future Forms

Rewrite in Italian.

1. I won't eat _____
2. He won't listen _____
3. We won't drink _____
4. They won't eat _____

Chapter 4

Imperfect

1. Uses of the Imperfect

This is a very easy tense to learn, but not so easy to use.

In Italian, the *imperfect* is always used to refer to an action in the past that is continuing while another takes place.

| **Example:** | Mentre *parlavo,* tu arrivasti. | While I *was speaking,* you came. |

The *imperfect tense* in Italian expresses the English *used to.*

| **Example:** | *Parlavo.* | I used to speak. |

With verbs of *thinking, believing,* and *feeling,* the imperfect is generally used rather than the other past forms—the *past definite (passato remoto)* or the *present perfect (passato prossimo),* found in future lessons.

| **Examples:** | *Volevo* scrivere. | I wanted to write. |
| | Mi *sentivo* male. | I felt bad. |

The *imperfect* is used to describe actions or conditions that lasted for an indefinite period of time in the past. In English, this is the same as the form expressed by *was* and the *ing* form of the verb.

| **Examples:** | *Leggevo* il giornale. | I *was reading* the newspaper. |
| | *Guardavo* la televisione. | I *was watching* television. |

The *imperfect* is used to express habitual action in the past, and it is usually preceded or followed by words such as *di solito, qualche volta, spesso, sempre.*

| **Examples:** | *Studiava sempre* con la sua amica. | She used to always study with her friend. |
| | Di solito, *guardavo* la televisione. | Usually, I would watch TV. |

The *imperfect* tense is used to describe time, age, weather, in the past.

| **Example:** | *Faceva* bel tempo/brutto tempo. | The weather was nice/bad. |

2. Forms of the Imperfect

The *imperfect* is formed by adding the same endings to all three conjugations. The only difference among the conjugations is the typical vowel of the infinitive.

parlare—parl*avo*   (To speak—I used to speak)
credere—cred*evo*   (To believe—I used to believe)
finire—fin*ivo*   (To finish—I used to finish)

Parlare To speak	**Vedere** To see	**Dormire** To sleep
io parl*avo*	io ved*evo*	io dorm*ivo*
tu parl*avi*	tu ved*evi*	tu dorm*ivi*
lui parl*ava*	lui ved*eva*	lui dorm*iva*
lei parl*ava*	lei ved*eva*	lei dorm*iva*
noi parl*avamo*	noi ved*evamo*	noi dorm*ivamo*
voi parl*avate*	voi ved*evate*	voi dorm*ivate*
loro parl*avano*	loro ved*evano*	loro dorm*ivano*

3. Practice

Write the *imperfect tense* of the verbs.

1. **pensare**   io _____   tu _____   lui, lei _____
   (to think)   noi _____   voi _____   loro _____

2. **bere**   io _____   tu _____   lui, lei _____
   (to drink)   noi _____   voi _____   loro _____

3. **finire**   io _____   tu _____   lui, lei _____
   (to finish)   noi _____   voi _____   loro _____

4. **abitare**   io _____   tu _____   lui, lei _____
   (to live)   noi _____   voi _____   loro _____

4. Practice

Write the verbs in the *imperfect tense* in the person indicated.

Io:

mangiare   mettere   sentire

_____   _____   _____

Tu:

cantare   vedere   finire

_____   _____   _____

Lui, Lei:

saltare   bere   aprire

_____   _____   _____

Noi:

votare   rispondere   costruire

_____   _____   _____

Voi:

giocare   comprendere   applaudire

_____   _____   _____

Loro:

sperare   vendere   preferire

_____   _____   _____

5. Practice

A. Write the *imperfect* of the verbs.

1. Lui (parlare) _____
2. Voi (cantare)_____
3. Lui (abitare) _____
4. Noi (partire) _____
5. Voi (giocare) _____
6. Loro (finire) _____
7. Io (camminare)_____
8. Tu (perdere) _____
9. Voi (comprendere) _____
10. Loro (mangiare) _____
11. Tu (costruire) _____
12. Voi (istruire) _____
13. Lui (lavorare) _____
14. Lei (ballare) _____
15. Loro (pensare) _____
16. Voi (credere) _____
17. Tu (lavare) _____
18. Noi (scrivere) _____
19. Io (correre) _____
20. Lei (parlare) _____

B. Rewrite in English.

1. Mangiavamo _____
2. Studiavi_____
3. Bevevi_____
4. Giocavi _____
5. Sentiva _____
6. Capivate _____
7. Scrivevano _____
8. Chiedevo_____
9. Chiudevate _____
10. Ascoltava _____
11. Prendevamo _____
12. Imparavo_____
13. Vendevamo_____
14. Vendevi_____
15. Capivi _____
16. Vivevano_____
17. Istruiva _____
18. Vedeva _____
19. Ricevevano _____
20. Insegnavo _____

6. Practice

Rewrite in Italian, using the *imperfect.*

1. They used to eat _____
2. We were thinking_____
3. You (s.) were coming _____
4. I believed _____
5. They didn't think _____
6. I was learning _____
7. They believed_____
8. We used to ask _____
9. You (s.) didn't want _____
10. He was waiting _____
11. They were learning _____
12. I understood _____
13. You could _____
14. We used to sing _____
15. They wanted_____
16. I thought _____
17. We thought_____
18. He wanted_____
19. He used to go_____
20. I was waiting _____
21. I was hoping _____
22. We used to hope _____
23. I used to speak_____

24. Were you studying?_____
25. Were you speaking?_____
26. He was hoping _____
27. You (s.) thought_____
28. We were working _____
29. They wanted_____
30. We used to look_____
31. Were we looking? _____
32. He used to travel _____
33. I was teaching _____
34. They used to eat _____
35. I didn't understand_____
36. I couldn't _____
37. They used to sing _____
38. They didn't want _____
39. I didn't think _____
40. You (s.) thought_____
41. She wanted _____
42. I used to clean _____
43. We were looking _____
44. They weren't hoping _____
45. He was hoping_____
46. You (s.) doubted _____

Passato Remoto (Preterit)

7. Uses of the Passato Remoto

The *passato remoto* is a past tense, also called the historical past. It is mostly used in narrative writing of events of the past.

The *passato remoto* and the *passato prossimo* (a compound tense found in the next chapter) are similar since they both express an action in the past. They are commonly translated into English by the simple past, e.g., I bought, we played.

The *passato prossimo* is commonly used in speaking about the past. On the other hand, the *passato remoto* is mostly used in writing but is sometimes used in speaking, when the action is considered distant and not connected to the present.

8. Forms of the Passato Remoto

The *passato remoto* is formed by putting the correct endings to the infinitive roots. Following are the endings of the *passato remoto* for the three conjugations. Many common verbs have irregular roots for the *passato remoto.*

Comprare To buy	**Vendere** To sell	**Sentire** To hear
io compr*ai*	vend*ei*	sent*ii*
tu compr*asti*	vend*esti*	sent*isti*
lui compr*ò*	vend*è*	sent*ì*
lei compr*ò*	vend*è*	sent*ì*
noi compr*ammo*	vend*emmo*	sent*immo*
voi compr*aste*	vend*este*	sent*iste*
loro compr*arono*	vend*erono*	sent*irono*

9. Practice

Write the *passato remoto* of the verbs.

1. **mangiare**   io _____   tu _____   lui, lei _____
   (to eat)   noi _____   voi _____   loro _____

2. **potere**   io _____   tu _____   lui, lei _____
   (to be able)   noi _____   voi _____   loro _____

3. **capire**   io _____   tu _____   lui, lei _____
   (to understand) noi _____   voi _____   loro _____

10. Common Verbs with Irregular Roots in the Passato Remoto

Many common verbs have irregular roots in the *passato remoto* and they must be learned. The endings are the same as previously shown. Following are some of the most common verbs with irregular roots for the *passato remoto.*

Accendere: *Accesi, accendesti, accese, accendemmo, accendeste, accesero*

Bere: *Bevvi, bevesti, bevve, bevemmo, beveste, bevvero*

Cadere: *Caddi, cadesti, cadde, cademmo, cadeste, caddero*

Chiedere: *Chiesi, chiedesti, chiese, chiedemmo, chiedeste, chiesero*

Chiudere: *Chiusi, chiudesti, chiuse, chiudemmo, chiudeste, chiusero*

Cogliere: *Colsi, cogliesti, colse, cogliemmo, coglieste, colsero*

Conoscere: *Conobbi, conoscesti, conobbe, conoscemmo, conosceste, conobbero*

Dare: *Diedi, desti, diede, demmo, deste, diedero*

Decidere: *Decisi, decidesti, decise, decidemmo, decideste, decisero*

Dire: *Dissi, dicesti, disse, dicemmo, diceste, dissero*

Discutere: *Discussi, discutesti, discusse, discutemmo, discuteste, discussero*

Dovere: *Dovetti, dovesti, dovette, dovemmo, doveste, dovettero*

Fare: *Feci, facesti, fece, facemmo, faceste, fecero*

Leggere: *Lessi, leggesti, lesse, leggemmo, leggeste, lessero*

Mettere: *Misi, mettesti, mise, mettemmo, metteste, misero*

Nascere: *Nacqui, nascesti, nacque, nascemmo, nasceste, nacquero*

Prendere: *Presi, prendesti, prese, prendemmo, prendeste, presero*

Porre: *Posi, ponesti, pose, ponemmo, poneste, posero*

Ridere: *Risi, ridesti, rise, ridemmo, rideste, risero*

Rimanere: *Rimasi, rimanesti, rimase, rimanemmo, rimaneste, rimasero*

Sapere: *Seppi, sapesti, seppe, sapemmo, sapeste, seppero*

Scegliere: *Scelsi, scegliesti, scelse, scegliemmo, sceglieste, scelsero*

Scendere: *Scesi, scendesti, scese, scendemmo, scendeste, scesero*

Scrivere: *Scrissi, scrivesti, scrisse, scrivemmo, scriveste, scrissero*

Spegnere: *Spensi, spegnesti, spense, spegnemmo, spegneste, spensero*

Stare: *Stetti, stesti, stette, stemmo, steste, stettero*

Tenere: *Tenni, tenesti, tenne, tenemmo, teneste, tennero*

Vedere: *Vidi, vedesti, vide, vedemmo, vedeste, videro*

Venire: *Venni, venisti, venne, venimmo, veniste, vennero*

Vincere: *Vinsi, vincesti, vinse, vincemmo, vinceste, vinsero*

Vivere: *Vissi, vivesti, visse, vivemmo, viveste, vissero*

Volere: *Volli, volesti, volle, volemmo, voleste, vollero*

11. Practice

Write the *passato remoto* of the verbs in the person indicated.

Io:

chiedere   conoscere   sentire

_____   _____   _____

Tu:

comprare   temere   finire

_____   _____   _____

Carlo:

nascere   vedere   volere

_____   _____   _____

Maria:

capire   scrivere   venire

_____   _____   _____

Noi:

fare   bere   ridere

_____   _____   _____

Voi:

scendere   vincere   mettere

_____   _____   _____

Loro:

offrire   partire   fare

_____   _____   _____

12. Practice

Rewrite in English.

1. Io venni _____
2. Io risi _____
3. Io bevvi _____
4. Lui cadde _____
5. Lei chiese _____
6. Noi chiudemmo _____
7. Voi conosceste _____
8. Tu dicesti _____
9. Lei decise _____
10. Noi dicemmo _____
11. Voi doveste _____
12. Loro dissero _____
13. Io vissi _____
14. Loro vinsero _____
15. Tu facesti _____
16. Lei lesse _____
17. Noi leggemmo _____
18. Tu mettesti _____
19. Voi nasceste _____
20. Io presi _____

21. Noi prendemmo _____
22. Tu ridesti _____
23. Loro risero _____
24. Lei rimase _____
25. Tu scegliesti _____
26. Loro scrissero _____
27. Io scelsi _____
28. Tu scegliesti _____
29. Loro scrissero _____
30. Voi steste _____
31. Tu vedesti _____
32. Noi vedemmo _____
33. Voi vinceste _____
34. Io vidi _____
35. Loro videro _____
36. Lei visse _____
37. Lui volle _____
38. Noi volemmo _____
39. Loro vennero _____
40. Tu stesti _____

13. Review Practice

Practices 13 and 14 review the *present, imperative, imperfect, future,* and *passato remoto.*
Rewrite in English.

1. Parlo _____
2. Mangiamo _____
3. Abitano _____
4. Abitate? _____
5. Guidiamo _____
6. Non lavoro _____
7. Ritorneremo _____
8. Ritorneranno _____
9. Non volo _____
10. Volate? _____
11. Arriveranno _____
12. Arriverò _____
13. Non arriverete _____
14. Chiedo _____
15. Non chiedevo _____
16. Chiudono _____
17. Chiudi? _____
18. Penso _____
19. Penserai _____
20. Riposiamo _____
21. Riposano _____
22. Non riposi _____
23. Parlai _____
24. Pensammo _____
25. Riposi? _____
26. Mangia! _____
27. Guardate! _____
28. Parlate! _____
29. Impara! _____
30. Non guardare! _____
31. Non dormire! _____
32. Senta! _____
33. Prometti? _____
34. Risponderò _____
35. Scriveremo _____
36. Leggevo _____
37. Parlavi _____
38. Volevate _____
39. Piangevano _____
40. Insistevi _____
41. Bevevi _____
42. Bevi! _____
43. Bevete! _____
44. Non bere! _____
45. Vieni _____
46. Vieni? _____
47. Lesse _____
48. Sentiste _____

14. Review Practice

Rewrite in Italian.

1. They live _____

2. I used to open _____

3. They worked _____

4. We climb _____

5. I understand _____

6. They ate _____

7. We ate_____

8. He works _____

9. They study _____

10. I keep_____

11. I write _____

12. You (s.) used to write _____

13. I'll write _____

14. You (s.) travel_____

15. You (s.) used to travel _____

16. They'll travel _____

17. I leave_____

18. He leaves _____

19. We'll leave _____

20. She was leaving _____

21. He was learning _____

22. We were learning_____

23. They thought_____

24. I'll live _____

25. We'll open _____

26. Eat (s.)!_____

27. Work (s.)!_____

28. He'll eat _____

29. He'll work _____

30. Study (s.)!_____

31. Study (pl.)!_____

32. Drink (s.)!_____

33. Drink (pl.)!_____

34. We promised _____

35. I wanted _____

36. She must_____

37. Answer (s.)! _____

38. Write (s.) (formal)!_____

39. Speak (s.) (formal)! _____

40. I said_____

41. We'll wait_____

42. I discuss _____

43. We used to see_____

44. They know _____

45. We understand _____

46. I used to think _____

Chapter 5

Essere (To Be) and *Avere* (To Have)

1. Forms of *Essere* and *Avere*

It is important to become familiar with the irregular verbs **essere** and **avere,** two of the most commonly used verbs in Italian. Besides being used alone in the usual conjugations, they are also used to form the compound tenses.

Following are the complete conjugations of **essere** and **avere.** (Note that some of the tenses will be covered in later chapters.)

Essere	*Avere*
Present Indicative	
sono, sei, è, siamo, siete, sono	*ho, hai, ha, abbiamo, avete, hanno*
Imperfect	
ero, eri, era, eravamo,	*avevo, avevi, aveva, avevamo,*
eravate, erano	*avevate, avevano*
Future	
sarò, sarai, sarà, saremo,	*avrò, avrai, avrà, avremo,*
sarete, saranno	*avrete, avranno*
Imperative	
sii, siamo, siate	*abbi, abbiamo, abbiate*
sia (pol. s.), siano (pol. pl.)	*abbia (pol. s.), abbiano (pol. pl.)*
Passato Remoto (Preterit)	
fui, fosti, fu, fummo	*ebbi, avesti, ebbe, avemmo,*
foste, furono	*aveste, ebbero*
Passato Prossimo (Present Perfect)	
sono stato/a, sei stato/a, è stato/a,	*ho avuto, hai avuto, ha avuto,*
siamo stati/e, siete stati/e, sono stati/e	*abbiamo avuto, avete avuto,*
	hanno avuto
Trapassato Prossimo (Pluperfect)	
ero stato/a, eri stato/a, era stato/a,	*avevo avuto, avevi avuto, aveva*
eravamo stati/e, eravate stati/e,	*avuto, avevamo avuto, avevate*
erano stati/e	*avuto, avevano avuto*

Essere

Present Conditional
sarei, saresti, sarebbe, saremmo,
sareste, sarebbero

Past Conditional
sarei stato/a, saresti stato/a, sarebbe
stato/a, saremmo stati/e, sareste stati/e,
sarebbero stati/e

Present Subjunctive
che io sia, tu sia, lui/lei sia,
noi siamo, voi siate, loro siano

Imperfect Subjunctive
che io fossi, tu fossi,
lui/lei fosse,
noi fossimo, voi foste,
loro fossero

Past Subjunctive
che io sia stato/a, tu sia
stato/a, lui/lei sia stato/a,
noi siano stati/e, voi siate
stati/e, loro siano stati/e

Pluperfect Subjunctive
che io fossi stato/a, tu fossi stato/a,
lui/lei fosse stato/a,
noi fossimo stati/e, voi foste
stati/e, loro fossero stati/e

Avere

Present Conditional
avrei, avresti, avrebbe, avremmo,
avreste, avrebbero

Past Conditional
avrei avuto, avresti avuto,
avrebbe, avuto, avremmo avuto,
avreste avuto, avrebbero avuto

Present Subjunctive
che io abbia, tu abbia, lui/lei
abbia, noi abbiamo, voi abbiate,
loro abbiano

Imperfect Subjunctive
che io avessi, tu avessi,
lui/lei avesse,
noi avessimo, voi aveste,
loro avessero

Past Subjunctive
che io abbia avuto, tu abbia
avuto, lui/lei abbia avuto,
noi abbiamo avuto, voi abbiate
avuto, loro abbiano avuto

Pluperfect Subjunctive
che io avessi avuto, tu avessi
avuto, lui/lei avesse avuto,
noi avessimo avuto, voi aveste
avuto, loro avessero avuto

Passato Prossimo with *Avere*

2. Uses of the Passato Prossimo

The *passato prossimo* (present perfect) is used to describe actions and events that occurred in the recent past. It is often preceded or followed by such time expressions as *ieri, domenica scorsa, l'anno scorso, un anno fa, un'ora fa.*

3. Forms of the Passato Prossimo with *Avere*

The *passato prossimo* of most Italian verbs is formed by the present tense of the auxiliary verb *avere* and the past participle of the verb.

Examples:		
io	*ho mangiato*	I have eaten
tu	*hai mangiato*	you have eaten
lui	*ha mangiato*	he has eaten
lei	*ha mangiato*	she has eaten
noi	*abbiamo mangiato*	we have eaten
voi	*avete mangiato*	you have eaten
loro	*hanno mangiato*	they have eaten

The *past participle* is formed, for regular verbs, by adding:

  ato to the infinitive root of *-are* verbs
  uto to the infinitive root of *-ere* verbs
  ito to the infinitive root of *-ire* verbs

Infinitive:	*parlare* (to speak)	*vedere* (to see)	*sentire* (to hear)
Past Participle:	*parlato* (spoken)	*veduto* (seen)	*sentito* (heard)

In English, the *passato prossimo* is translated either with the simple past or the present perfect.

Examples:	*Ho mangiato* alle otto.	I *ate* at eight o'clock.
	Ho mangiato tardi.	I *have* eaten late.

Note: With the verb *avere,* the past participle doesn't agree in gender and number with the subject. The negative is formed by placing *non* in front of *avere.* If there is a second negative, this follows *avere.*

Examples:	*Non ho parlato* molto.	I didn't talk a lot.
	Non ho mai parlato molto.	I never talked a lot.

Passato Prossimo with *Essere*

4. Forms of the Passato Prossimo with *Essere*

The *passato prossimo* of several Italian verbs is formed with the auxiliary verb *essere* plus the past participle. The past participle agrees in gender and in number with the subject.

Examples:	Masculine		Feminine	
	io	sono andato	io	sono andata
	tu	sei andato	tu	sei andata
	lui	è andato	lei	è andata
	noi	siamo andati	noi	siamo andate
	voi	siete andati	voi	siete andate
	loro	sono andati	loro	sono andate

5. Common Verbs with *Essere* in the Passato Prossimo

Following is a list of commonly used verbs that form the *passato prossimo* with *essere.*

andare	to go	*Sono andato/a a scuola.*	I went to school.
arrivare	to arrive	*È arrivata tardi.*	She arrived late.
diventare	to become	*È diventato famoso.*	He became famous.
entrare	to enter	*Sono entrato/a.*	I went inside.
morire	to die	*Il cane è morto.*	The dog died.
nascere	to be born	*Sono nati/e ieri.*	They were born yesterday.
partire	to depart	*Gianni è già partito.*	John left already.
restare	to remain	*Lei è restata a casa.*	She remained at home.
rimanere	to remain	*Lui è rimasto a casa.*	He remained at home.
scendere	to descend	*Siamo scesi/e in fretta.*	We descended in a hurry.
stare	to stay	*Sono state a casa.*	They stayed home.
tornare	to return	*Siete tornati tardi.*	You returned late.
uscire	to go out	*È appena uscito.*	He just went out.
venire	to come	*Sono venuto/a in America.*	I came to America.

Irregular Past Participles

6. List of Irregular Past Participles

Many Italian verbs, especially *-ere* verbs, have irregular past participles.

Following is a list of the most common verbs with irregular *past participles:*

Infinitive		Past Participle
accadere	to happen	*accaduto*
accendere	to turn on	*acceso*
aggiungere	to add	*aggiunto*
apparire	to appear	*apparso*
appendere	to hang	*appeso*
apprendere	to learn	*appreso*
aprire	to open	*aperto*
assumere	to hire	*assunto*
bere	to drink	*bevuto*
chiedere	to ask	*chiesto*
chiudere	to close	*chiuso*
cogliere	to gather	*colto*
comprendere	to comprehend	*compreso*
concludere	to conclude	*concluso*
confondere	to confuse	*confuso*
conoscere	to know	*conosciuto*
convincere	to convince	*convinto*
coprire	to cover	*coperto*
correre	to run	*corso*
correggere	to correct	*corretto*
cuocere	to cook	*cotto*
decidere	to decide	*deciso*
difendere	to defend	*difeso*
dire	to tell, say	*detto*
discutere	to discuss	*discusso*
distinguere	to distinguish	*distinto*
dividere	to divide	*diviso*
eleggere	to elect	*eletto*
esprimere	to express	*espresso*
fare	to make, do	*fatto*
includere	to include	*incluso*
interrompere	to interrupt	*interrotto*
leggere	to read	*letto*

Infinitive		Past Participle
mettere	to put	*messo*
morire	to die	*morto*
muovere	to move	*mosso*
nascere	to be born	*nato*
nascondere	to hide	*nascosto*
offrire	to offer	*offerto*
perdere	to lose	*perso*
permettere	to permit	*permesso*
prendere	to take, get	*preso*
promettere	to promise	*promesso*
promuovere	to promote	*promosso*
proporre	to propose	*proposto*
porre	to put	*posto*
proteggere	to protect	*protetto*
provvedere	to provide	*provvisto*
raggiungere	to reach	*raggiunto*
richiedere	to request	*richiesto*
ridere	to laugh	*riso*
ridurre	to reduce	*ridotto*
rimanere	to remain	*rimasto*
rimuovere	to remove	*rimosso*
risolvere	to resolve	*risolto*
rispondere	to answer	*risposto*
rompere	to break	*rotto*
scegliere	to choose	*scelto*
scendere	to descend	*sceso*
scomparire	to disappear	*scomparso*
scrivere	to write	*scritto*
soffrire	to suffer	*sofferto*
sorridere	to smile	*sorriso*
spegnere	to turn off	*spento*
spendere	to spend	*speso*
spingere	to push	*spinto*
succedere	to happen	*successo*
togliere	to remove	*tolto*
trasmettere	to broadcast	*trasmesso*
vedere	to see	*visto*
vincere	to win	*vinto*
vivere	to live	*vissuto*

7. Practice

Write the *passato prossimo* of the verbs.

1. **mangiare** io _____ tu _____ lui, lei _____

   (to eat) noi _____ voi _____ loro _____

2. **scrivere** io _____ tu _____ lui, lei _____

   (to write) noi _____ voi _____ loro _____

3. **venire** io _____ tu _____ lui, lei _____

   (to come) noi _____ voi _____ loro _____

4. **andare** io _____ tu _____ lui, lei _____

   (to go) noi _____ voi _____ loro _____

8. Practice

Write the verb in the *passato prossimo* in the person indicated.

Io:

mangiare	vedere	sentire

Tu:

parlare	scrivere	capire

Lui:

viaggiare	potere	finire

Lei:

camminare	volere	venire

Noi:

lodare	spingere	salire

Voi:

stare	ridere	aprire

Loro:

dare	rimanere	nutrire

Carlo:

fare	nascere	offrire

Maria:

andare	nascondere	pulire

Io e Giovanni:

aspettare	vendere	partire

Tu e Pietro:

imparare	chiudere	uscire

Giovanni e Paolo:

fermare	vivere	finire

9. Practice

Write the verbs in the *passato prossimo*, using the negative in the person indicated.

Io:

essere   avere   potere

_____   _____   _____

Tu:

volere   dovere   capire

_____   _____   _____

Lui:

fare   dare   stare

_____   _____   _____

Noi:

andare   arrivare   partire

_____   _____   _____

10. Practice

Write the verbs in the *passato prossimo* in the person indicated by the subject.

1. Lui (parlare) _____
2. Noi (stare)_____
3. Lei (stare) _____
4. Voi (leggere)_____
5. Loro (sentire) _____
6. Io (dormire)_____
7. Tu (perdere) _____
8. Lei (andare)_____
9. Lui (decidere) _____
10. Noi (comprare)_____
11. Voi (vivere) _____
12. Loro (bere) _____
13. Lui (parlare) _____
14. Lei (aprire) _____
15. Lui (aprire) _____
16. Voi (imparare) _____
17. Noi (temere) _____
18. Io (mangiare) _____
19. Tu (ricevere)_____
20. Lui (lavorare) _____
21. Noi (viaggiare) _____
22. Loro (potere)_____
23. Voi (insegnare)_____
24. Noi (sciare)_____
25. Noi (correre)_____
26. Io (guardare)_____
27. Tu (guarire)_____
28. Voi (rispondere) _____
29. Loro (arrivare) _____
30. Noi (tenere) _____
31. Lei (vendere) _____
32. Loro (vivere) _____
33. Io (abitare) _____
34. Noi (gettare) _____

11. Practice

Write the verbs in the *passato prossimo,* using the negative in the person indicated.

1. Lui (mangiare) _____
2. Lei (comprare) _____
3. Tu (parlare)_____
4. Io (studiare) _____
5. Loro (dovere) _____
6. Noi (cantare)_____
7. Loro (vedere) _____
8. Voi (sentire) _____
9. Tu (scrivere)_____
10. Noi (volere) _____

12. Practice

Rewrite in Italian, using the *passato prossimo.*

1. We answered _____

2. They bought _____

3. We learned _____

4. She bought _____

5. I asked _____

6. You (s.) answered _____

7. We left _____

8. I drank _____

9. I didn't drink _____

10. They taught _____

11. I read_____

12. You (s.) wrote _____

13. They worked _____

14. He slept _____

15. She worked _____

16. We studied _____

17. He didn't ski _____

18. She didn't go _____

19. She was born _____

20. They sold _____

21. I didn't listen _____

22. I didn't hear _____

23. I didn't ask _____

24. You (s.) didn't answer_____

25. I received _____

26. I learned _____

27. They understood_____

28. She traveled _____

29. We didn't travel _____

30. They cleaned _____

31. We thought _____

32. They didn't think _____

33. I cleaned _____

34. You (s.) paid _____

35. You (s.) didn't pay_____

36. We ate_____

37. I arrived _____

38. They stayed _____

Trapassato Prossimo

13. Forms of the Trapassato Prossimo

The *trapassato prossimo* (pluperfect) is formed by using the imperfect of the auxiliary verbs *avere* or *essere,* plus the *past participle.*

Examples:	*avevo mangiato*	I had eaten	*ero andato/a*	I had gone
	avevi mangiato	you had eaten	*eri andato/a*	you had gone
	aveva mangiato	he had eaten	*era andato*	he had gone
	aveva mangiato	she had eaten	*era andata*	she had gone
	avevamo mangiato	we had eaten	*eravamo andati/e*	we had gone
	avevate mangiato	you had eaten	*eravate andati/e*	you had gone
	avevano mangiato	they had eaten	*erano andati/e*	they had gone

14. Uses of the Trapassato Prossimo

This tense is used to express an action in the past that had happened before another one. The more recent past action can be expressed in the *passato prossimo, passato remoto,* or *imperfect.*

Examples:	Dove è stato Giulio?	Where did Giulio go?
	È andato in vacanza	He went on vacation
	dove *era stato* tanti	where he had been
	anni fa.	many years ago.

15. Practice

Write the *trapassato prossimo* of the verbs.

1. **guardare**   io _____   tu _____   lui, lei _____
   (to look)   noi _____   voi _____   loro _____

2. **vedere**   io _____   tu _____   lui, lei _____
   (to see)   noi _____   voi _____   loro _____

3. **partire**   io _____   tu _____   lui, lei _____
   (to leave)   noi _____   voi _____   loro _____

16. Practice

Write the verbs in the *trapassato prossimo* in the person indicated.

Io:
mangiare   vedere   sentire

_____   _____   _____

Tu:
parlare   credere   pulire

_____   _____   _____

Lui, Lei:
visitare   scrivere   finire

_____   _____   _____

Noi:
arrivare   bere   capire

_____   _____   _____

Voi:
comprare   leggere   venire

_____   _____   _____

Loro:
dare   potere   aprire

_____   _____   _____

Carlo:
giocare   spingere   costruire

_____   _____   _____

Carlo e Maria:
viaggiare   vendere   partire

_____   _____   _____

17. Practice

Rewrite in Italian, using the *trapassato prossimo.*

1. I had understood   _____

2. You had gone   _____

3. She had studied   _____

4. He had drunk   _____

5. We had finished   _____

6. You (pl.) had slept   _____

7. They had bought   _____

8. I had worked   _____

9. You (s.) had thought   _____

10. He had played   _____

11. We had traveled   _____

12. You (pl.) had cleaned   _____

13. They had watched   _____

14. I had been   _____

15. You (s.) had arrived   _____

16. He had left   _____

17. She had gone   _____

18. We had read   _____

19. You (pl.) had written   _____

20. They had finished   _____

21. I had won   _____

22. He had lost   _____

23. She had gone   _____

24. We had listened   _____

18. Review Practice

This practice reviews the *passato prossimo* and *trapassato prossimo*.

Rewrite in Italian.

1. I have eaten _____

2. You (s.) had eaten _____

3. She has gone _____

4. He had come _____

5. We have finished _____

6. We had finished _____

7. You (pl.) have seen _____

8. You (pl.) had looked _____

9. They have read _____

10. They had read _____

11. I have played _____

12. I had slept _____

13. He has eaten _____

14. We had skied _____

15. We have not read _____

16. We had not thought _____

17. They have not won _____

18. They had not promised _____

19. I have not chosen _____

20. He has not come _____

21. She had not left _____

22. We have lived _____

23. We have not lived _____

24. We had lived _____

Chapter 6

Conditional

1. Uses of the Conditional

The conditional *(condizionale)* is used to refer to an action or state that *may* happen if something else occurred or if some condition were present. In English, the conditional is indicated by *would.*

Example: Al tuo posto *studierei* di più.   In your place I would study more.

The conditional is used to add politeness or kindness to wishes and demands.

Examples: *Vorrei* un caffè.   I would like a coffee.
   Mi *faresti* un favore?   Would you do me a favor?

2. Forms of the Conditional

The *present conditional* tense is made up of the future root plus the conditional endings, which are the same for all three conjugations.

Cantare (To sing)	**Vendere** (To sell)	**Sentire** (To hear)
io cant*erei*	vend*erei*	sent*irei*
tu cant*eresti*	vend*eresti*	sent*iresti*
lui cant*erebbe*	vend*erebbe*	sent*irebbe*
lei cant*erebbe*	vend*erebbe*	sent*irebbe*
noi cant*eremmo*	vend*eremmo*	sent*iremmo*
voi cant*ereste*	vend*ereste*	sent*ireste*
loro cant*erebbero*	vend*erebbero*	sent*irebbero*

Note: Remember the use of *e* in the stem for *-are* verbs.

Verbs ending in *-care* and *-gare* add an *h* in the conditional to keep the hard *c* and *g* sounds: *pagherei, giocherei.*

Verbs ending in *-ciare* and *-giare* drop the *i* in the conditional: *comincerei, mangerei.*

Verbs that have irregular roots in the future use the same irregular roots in the conditional. Following are the most common verbs that have irregular roots:

andare	*andr*	*andrei, andresti, etc.*
bere	*berr*	*berrei, berresti, etc.*
cadere	*cadr*	*cadrei, cadresti, etc.*
dare	*dar*	*darei, daresti, etc.*
dovere	*dovr*	*dovrei, dovresti, etc.*
essere	*sar*	*sarei, saresti, etc.*
fare	*far*	*farei, faresti, etc.*
potere	*potr*	*potrei, potresti, etc.*
sapere	*sapr*	*saprei, sapresti, etc.*
valere	*varr*	*varrei, varresti, etc.*
vedere	*vedr*	*vedrei, vedresti, etc.*
venire	*verr*	*verrei, verresti, etc.*
volere	*vorr*	*vorrei, vorresti, etc.*

Note: The conditional of *dovere* is translated as **should.**

3. Practice

Write the *present conditional* of the verbs.

1. **andare**   io _____   tu _____   lui, lei _____

   (to go)   noi _____   voi _____   loro _____

2. **dovere**   io _____   tu _____   lui, lei _____

   (to have to, must) noi _____ voi _____ loro _____

3. **venire**   io _____   tu _____   lui, lei _____

   (to come)   noi _____   voi _____   loro _____

4. Practice

Write the verbs in the *present conditional* in the person indicated.

Io:

cantare   potere   capire

_____   _____   _____

Tu:

ballare   vedere   dormire

_____   _____   _____

Lui, Lei:

nuotare   bere   sentire

_____   _____   _____

Noi:

ordinare   leggere   finire

_____   _____   _____

Voi:

viaggiare   dovere   partire

_____   _____   _____

Loro:

domandare   volere   venire

_____   _____   _____

Giovanna:

ascoltare   avere   dire

_____   _____   _____

Io e Carlo:

parlare   vedere   colpire

_____   _____   _____

Tu e Giovanna:

desiderare   vincere   ubbidire

_____   _____   _____

Giovanna e Carlo:

organizzare   promettere   offrire

_____   _____   _____

5. Practice

Write the verbs in the *negative* of the *present conditional.*

Io:

parlare   vedere   sentire

_____   _____   _____

Tu:

viaggiare   scrivere   pulire

_____   _____   _____

Paolo:

mangiare   potere   capire

_____   _____   _____

Io e Carlo:

studiare   leggere   finire

_____   _____   _____

Tu e Paolo:

arrivare   volere   partire

_____   _____   _____

6. Practice

Rewrite in English.

1. Comprerei _____
2. Vedresti _____
3. Capirei _____
4. Non mangeremmo _____
5. Verreste _____
6. Sentirebbero _____
7. Studierei _____
8. Non studierei _____
9. Viaggeresti _____
10. Capirebbe _____
11. Carla arriverebbe _____
12. Saremmo _____
13. Scriverebbero _____
14. Dormirei _____
15. Non leggeresti _____
16. Paolo non partirebbe _____
17. Faremmo _____
18. Non giochereste _____
19. Sareste _____
20. Ascolterebbero _____
21. Verrei _____
22. Non verrei _____
23. Staresti _____
24. Carlo capirebbe _____
25. Maria cucinerebbe _____
26. Giocheremmo _____
27. Vorremmo _____
28. Non vorremmo _____
29. Tu e Paolo fareste _____
30. Non farei _____
31. Andremmo _____
32. Portereste _____
33. Carla non porterebbe _____
34. Dovrebbero _____
35. Inviterei _____
36. Verrebbero _____

Interrogative Forms

1. Verresti? _____
2. Canterebbero? _____
3. Capirebbe? _____
4. Dareste? _____
5. Parlerebbe? _____
6. Sentiresti? _____
7. Faremmo? _____
8. Cucineresti? _____

7. Practice

Rewrite in Italian, using the *present conditional.*

1. I would think _____
2. I would drink _____
3. You could _____
4. He would do _____
5. He would not do _____
6. She would write _____
7. I would work _____
8. They would drink _____
9. I would clean _____
10. She would make _____
11. They would wash _____
12. I would watch _____
13. They would see _____
14. We would think _____
15. I would wash _____
16. You (s.) would understand _____
17. They would not go _____
18. You (pl.) would see _____
19. I would not take _____
20. I would know _____
21. You (s.) would go _____
22. You (s.) could not _____
23. She would think _____
24. We would write _____
25. They would read _____
26. I would sleep _____
27. They could not _____
28. We would eat _____
29. I would drink _____
30. You (pl.) would travel _____
31. She would return _____
32. He would arrive _____
33. They would leave _____
34. I would not arrive _____
35. She would not plant _____
36. He would win _____
37. They would eat _____
38. We would swim _____
39. You (pl.) would ski _____
40. We would look _____

8. Practice

Rewrite in Italian. Use the conditional of *dovere.*

1. I should go _____
2. You (s.) should write _____
3. They should study _____
4. We should come _____
5. He should cook _____
6. She should read _____

Past Conditional

9. Forms of the Past Conditional

The *past conditional (condizionale passato)* is a compound tense. It is formed by the conditional tense of the auxiliary *avere* or *essere* plus the past participle of the main verb. The past participle agrees with the subject when the verb is conjugated with the auxiliary *essere.*

10. Uses of the Past Conditional

The *past conditional* is used in dependent clauses to express an action that is considered future as viewed from the past. In English the present conditional is used, but in Italian the past conditional is used.

Example: Ha detto che **avrebbe scritto.**   He said that he would write (he would have written).

The *condizionale passato* of *dovere* followed by an infinitive expresses an obligation that was not done.

Example: *Avresti dovuto scrivere*   You should have written
     a tua mamma.   to your mother.

The *condizionale passato* is also used in sentences with *se* clauses. These will be studied in the next chapter.

11. Practice

Write the *past conditional* of the verbs.

1. **parlare**   io _____   tu _____   lui, lei _____
   (to speak)   noi _____   voi _____   loro _____

2. **vedere**   io _____   tu _____   lui, lei _____
   (to see)   noi _____   voi _____   loro _____

3. **venire**   io _____   tu _____   lui, lei _____
   (to come)   noi _____   voi _____   loro _____

12. Practice

Write the verbs in the *past conditional* in the person indicated.

Io:

andare	ritornare	partire
_____	_____	_____

Tu:

parlare	vedere	capire
_____	_____	_____

Lui, Lei:

arrivare	scrivere	dormire
_____	_____	_____

Noi:

informare	leggere	preferire
_____	_____	_____

Voi:

aspettare	dovere	finire
_____	_____	_____

Loro:

abitare	bere	uscire
_____	_____	_____

Carlo:

invitare	volere	sentire
_____	_____	_____

13. Review Practice

Practices 13 and 14 review the *present conditional* and the *past conditional.*
Rewrite in English.

1. Io avrei aspettato _____
2. Tu parleresti _____
3. Avrebbe mangiato _____
4. Capirebbero _____
5. Scrivereste _____
6. Avreste scritto _____
7. Risponderebbero _____
8. Non avrebbe risposto _____
9. Sentirei _____
10. Avrei sentito _____
11. Avremmo firmato _____
12. Inviterei _____
13. Uscireste _____
14. Finiremmo _____
15. Avrebbero finito _____
16. Comprereste _____
17. (Lui) comprerebbe _____
18. Troveresti _____
19. Avrei guardato _____
20. Risponderebbe _____
21. Avrebbe risposto _____
22. Avreste scritto _____
23. Saprei _____
24. Avrebbe saputo _____

14. Review Practice

Rewrite in Italian.

1. I would go _____

2. You (s.) would have taken _____

3. We would have danced _____

4. They would have come _____

5. She would know _____

6. We would wait _____

7. We would have started _____

8. She would write _____

9. He would have answered _____

10. They would speak _____

11. They should have come _____

12. I should have spoken _____

13. She should wait _____

14. She should have waited _____

15. We would understand _____

16. They would have understood _____

17. She would have written _____

18. You (s.) would have answered _____

19. You (s.) should have answered _____

20. They would travel _____

21. I would have returned _____

22. He would have left _____

23. She would arrive _____

24. We would leave _____

Chapter 7

Present Subjunctive

1. Uses of the Subjunctive

The subjunctive *(congiuntivo)* is used very frequently in Italian, while in English it is used very rarely. In Italian, the subjunctive is generally used in a dependent *che* clause and reflects the wishes, hopes, emotions, opinions, feelings, and doubts of the subject.

It is used mainly after the following verbs: ***pensare, credere, sperare, dubitare, non sapere, avere paura, volere.*** The verb in the main clause is in the indicative, and the *che* clause is in the subjunctive.

Examples:	Spero *che tu venga.*	I hope that you come.
	Vogliono *che io venga.*	They want me to come.

If there is no change of subject, the infinitive is used instead of the subjunctive after the verbs. The preposition *di* is used with certain verbs such as ***sperare, avere voglia, avere paura.***

Examples:	*Ho voglia di andare.*	I have a desire to go.
	Spero di vederlo.	I hope to see him/it.

2. Forms of the Present Subjunctive

The *present subjunctive* is formed by putting the endings of the subjunctive on the infinitive root. Following are the conjugations of the present subjunctive of regular *-are, -ere, -ire* verbs.

Che + pronoun	Parlare	Vedere	Sentire
che io	parl*i*	ved*a*	sent*a*
che tu	parl*i*	ved*a*	sent*a*
che lui	parl*i*	ved*a*	sent*a*
che lei	parl*i*	ved*a*	sent*a*
che noi	parl*iamo*	ved*iamo*	sent*iamo*
che voi	parl*iate*	ved*iate*	sent*iate*
che loro	parl*ino*	ved*ano*	sent*ano*

It is important in this tense to use the personal pronouns for the first three persons if the subject is unclear.

Example:	Penso *che lui capisca.*	I think that he understands.

The verbs in *-care* and *-gare* add an *h* in all forms of the present subjunctive.

	Giocare (To play)		**Pagare** (To pay)
che io	gio**chi**	che io	pag**hi**
che tu	gio**chi**	che io	pag**hi**
che lui	gio**chi**	che lui	pag**hi**
che lei	gio**chi**	che lei	pag**hi**
che noi	gio**chiamo**	che noi	pag**hiamo**
che voi	gio**chiate**	che voi	pag**hiate**
che loro	gio**chino**	che loro	pag**hino**

Examples are listed with the headings **Giocare** (To play) and **Pagare** (To pay).

The verbs in *-ciare* and *-giare* do not repeat the *i.*

Examples:

	Cominciare (To begin, start)		**Mangiare** (To eat)
che io	cominc**i**	che io	mang**i**
che tu	cominc**i**	che tu	mang**i**
che lui	cominc**i**	che lui	mang**i**
che lei	cominc**i**	che lei	mang**i**
che noi	cominc**iamo**	che noi	mang**iamo**
che voi	cominc**iate**	che voi	mang**iate**
che loro	cominc**ino**	che loro	mang**ino**

Verbs of the *-ire* conjugation with *isc* add an *-isc* between the root and the ending in all the singular persons and the 3rd person plural.

Example:

Che + pronoun	**Finire** (to finish)
che io	fin**isca**
che tu	fin**isca**
che lui	fin**isca**
che lei	fin**isca**
che noi	fin**iamo**
che voi	fin**iate**
che loro	fin**iscano**

The following commonly used verbs have irregular forms in the *present subjunctive.* All the endings have the vowel *a* regardless of whether they are *-are, -ere,* or *-ire* verbs.

andare	*vada, vada, vada, andiamo, andiate, vadano*
avere	*abbia, abbia, abbia, abbiamo, abbiate, abbiano*
bere	*beva, beva, beva, beviamo, beviate, bevano*
dare	*dia, dia, dia, diamo, diate, diano*
dire	*dica, dica, dica, diciamo, diciate, dicano*
dovere	*debba, debba, debba, dobbiamo, dobbiate, debbano*
essere	*sia, sia, sia, siamo, siate, siano*
fare	*faccia, faccia, faccia, facciamo, facciate, facciano*
potere	*possa, possa, possa, possiamo, possiate, possano*
rimanere	*rimanga, rimanga, rimanga, rimaniamo, rimaniate, rimangano*
sapere	*sappia, sappia, sappia, sappiamo, sappiate, sappiano*
stare	*stia, stia, stia, stiamo, stiate, stiano*
uscire	*esca, esca, esca, usciamo, usciate, escano*
venire	*venga, venga, venga, veniamo, veniate, vengano*
volere	*voglia, voglia, voglia, vogliamo, vogliate, vogliano*

3. The Subjunctive after Impersonal Expressions

The *present subjunctive* is used in a dependent *che* clause after impersonal expressions of possibility, opinion, and probability.

    Example: *È necessario che tu venga.*   It is necessary that you come.

Here are some impersonal expressions with which the subjunctive is used:

È necessario	It is necessary
È probabile	It is probable
È opportuno	It is opportune
È improbabile	It is improbable
È bene	It is good
È meglio	It is better
È giusto	It is right
È importante	It is important
È preferibile	It is preferable

If the impersonal verb indicates certainty, the subjunctive is not used.

    Example: *È certo che vengono oggi.*   It is certain they are coming today.

The impersonal expressions can also be followed by the infinitive with no subject indicated.

    Example: *È necessario studiare.*   It is necessary to study.

4. Practice

1. **domandare**   che io＿＿＿＿＿＿   che tu＿＿＿＿＿＿   che lui, lei ＿＿＿＿＿＿
   (to ask)   che noi＿＿＿＿＿＿   che voi＿＿＿＿＿＿   che loro ＿＿＿＿＿＿

2. **vedere**   che io＿＿＿＿＿＿   che tu＿＿＿＿＿＿   che lui, lei ＿＿＿＿＿＿
   (to see)   che noi＿＿＿＿＿＿   che voi＿＿＿＿＿＿   che loro ＿＿＿＿＿＿

3. **sentire**   che io＿＿＿＿＿＿   che tu＿＿＿＿＿＿   che lui, lei ＿＿＿＿＿＿
   (to hear)   che noi＿＿＿＿＿＿   che voi＿＿＿＿＿＿   che loro ＿＿＿＿＿＿

4. **capire**   che io＿＿＿＿＿＿   che tu＿＿＿＿＿＿   che lui, lei ＿＿＿＿＿＿
   (to understand) che noi＿＿＿＿＿＿   che voi＿＿＿＿＿＿   che loro ＿＿＿＿＿＿

5. **giocare**   che io＿＿＿＿＿＿   che tu＿＿＿＿＿＿   che lui, lei ＿＿＿＿＿＿
   (to play)   che noi＿＿＿＿＿＿   che voi＿＿＿＿＿＿   che loro ＿＿＿＿＿＿

6. **pagare**   che io＿＿＿＿＿＿   che tu＿＿＿＿＿＿   che lui, lei ＿＿＿＿＿＿
   (to pay)   che noi＿＿＿＿＿＿   che voi＿＿＿＿＿＿   che loro ＿＿＿＿＿＿

5. Practice

Write the verbs in the *present subjunctive* in the person indicated.

Che io:

domandare   decidere   sentire

_____   _____   _____

Che tu:

comprare   vedere   finire

_____   _____   _____

Che lui:

preparare   leggere   capire

_____   _____   _____

Che lei:

aspettare   comprendere   pulire

_____   _____   _____

Che noi:

arrivare   accendere   dire

_____   _____   _____

Che voi:

visitare   bere   partire

_____   _____   _____

Che loro:

lavorare   chiudere   capire

_____   _____   _____

6. Practice

Write the verbs in the *present subjunctive* in the person indicated or in the *infinitive*.

Io voglio che tu:

mangiare   leggere   partire

_____   _____   _____

Io voglio che lui:

parlare   perdere   offrire

_____   _____   _____

Io voglio che lei:

stare   discutere   aprire

_____   _____   _____

Io spero che noi:

imparare   sorridere   capire

_____   _____   _____

Io desidero che voi:

fare   vedere   ridere

_____   _____   _____

Io penso che loro:

desiderare   dovere   ubbidire

_____   _____   _____

Io voglio:

visitare   vincere   capire

_____   _____   _____

Loro vogliono:

visitare   arrivare   partire

_____   _____   _____

7. Practice

Choose the correct form of the verb from those in parentheses.

1. Mio padre vuole che io (legga, leggo) _____

2. Speriamo che i ragazzi (studiano, studino) _____

3. Spero che loro (comprano, comprino) _____

4. Penso che lui (capisce, capisca) _____

5. È necessario che io (vengo, venga) _____

6. È possibile che loro (arrivano, arrivino) _____

7. Vuole che tu (finisci, finisca) _____

8. Voglio che tu (vieni, venga) _____

9. Penso che tu (puoi, possa) _____

10. Credo che lui (legge, legga) _____

11. È bene che noi (veniamo, venire) _____

12. È possibile che voi (pensate, pensiate) _____

13. Credo di (sapere, sappia) _____

14. Spera che io (ritorni, ritorno) _____

15. Dubito che tu (sappia, so) _____

16. È bene che io (vado, vada) _____

17. Dubitiamo che lui (vince, vinca) _____

18. È possibile che lui (perda, perde) _____

19. È importante che loro (pensino, pensano) _____

20. È giusto che io (controlli, controllo) _____

21. È possibile che loro (possono, possano) _____

22. Ho voglia di (sapere, so) _____

23. Spero che loro (puliscano, puliscono) _____

24. Spera di (comprare, compri) _____

8. Practice

Change the verb from the *present indicative* to the *present subjunctive.*

1. Vado   _____

2. Sente (lui)   _____

3. Mangiamo   _____

4. Parlano   _____

5. Sentite   _____

6. Bevi   _____

7. Parte (lei)   _____

8. Capisce (lui)   _____

9. Lavoriamo   _____

10. Sentite   _____

11. Ascoltate   _____

12. Leggono   _____

13. Non ascoltate   _____

14. Andate   _____

15. Parto   _____

16. Arriva   _____

17. Piove   _____

18. So   _____

19. Conosci   _____

20. Puoi   _____

21. Non leggete   _____

22. Comprate   _____

23. Vendete   _____

24. Capite   _____

9. Practice

Rewrite the sentences, using the *present subjunctive* or *infinitive* of the verb in parentheses.

1. Io voglio che tu (andare)   _____

2. Spero di (partire)   _____

3. Dubitiamo che lui (arrivare)   _____

4. Dubitiamo che lei (pensare)   _____

5. Speri che io (visitare)   _____

6. Speri di (andare)   _____

7. Speriamo che lui (capire)   _____

8. Speriamo di (comprare)   _____

9. Pensate che io (vedere)   _____

10. Penso che tu (potere)   _____

11. Pensi che noi (volere)   _____

12. Dubito che tu (leggere)   _____

13. Speriamo di (finire)   _____

14. Sperano che io (pagare)   _____

15. Carlo vuole che io (ascoltare)   _____

16. Penso che Mario (comprare)   _____

17. Pensa che noi (vendere)   _____

18. Pensa che tu (scrivere)   _____

19. Penso che loro (guardare)   _____

20. Dubito che tu (studiare)   _____

21. È necessario che lui (partire)   _____

22. È possibile che noi (rimanere)   _____

23. Ho paura che voi (perdere)   _____

24. Voglio che tu (rimanere)   _____

Imperfect Subjunctive

10. Uses of the Imperfect Subjunctive

The imperfect subjunctive *(congiuntivo imperfetto),* like the present subjunctive, is used after certain verbs, impersonal expressions, and conjunctions. The main difference between these two tenses is the time of the action. If the action is in the present, the *present subjunctive* is used. If the action is related to the past, the *imperfect subjunctive* is used.

If the verb of the main clause is expressed in the past tense or conditional, the *imperfect subjunctive* is used in the dependent *che* clause.

Example: Paola pensava che *io arrivassi.*   Paola thought I would arrive.

11. Forms of the Imperfect Subjunctive

The *imperfect subjunctive* of all regular verbs and almost all irregular verbs is formed by adding the endings *ssi, ssi, sse, ssimo, ste, ssero* to the 1st person singular of the imperfect indicative after omitting the final **vo.**

Infinitive	Imperfect Indicative	Imperfect Subjunctive
Parlare	Parlavo	che io parlassi
Leggere	Leggevo	che io leggessi
Sentire	Sentivo	che io sentissi

The following chart shows the forms of the *imperfect subjunctive* of the regular *-are, -ere, -ire* verbs.

	Parlare	**Scrivere**	**Sentire**
che io	parla*ssi*	scrive*ssi*	senti*ssi*
che tu	parla*ssi*	scrive*ssi*	senti*ssi*
che lui	parla*sse*	scrive*sse*	senti*sse*
che lei	parla*sse*	scrive*sse*	senti*sse*
che noi	parla*ssimo*	scrive*ssimo*	senti*ssimo*
che voi	parla*ste*	scrive*ste*	senti*ste*
che loro	parla*ssero*	scrive*ssero*	senti*ssero*

The following verbs have *irregular* forms of the *imperfect subjunctive.*

stare	*stessi, stessi, stesse, stessimo, steste, stessero*
essere	*fossi, fossi, fosse, fossimo, foste, fossero*
dare	*dessi, dessi, desse, dessimo, deste, dessero*
dire	*dicessi, dicessi, dicesse, dicessimo, diceste, dicessero*
fare	*facessi, facessi, facesse, facessimo, faceste, facessero*

12. Practice

Write the *imperfect subjunctive* of the verbs.

1. **ascoltare** che io _____ che tu _____ che lui, lei _____

   (to listen) che noi _____ che voi _____ che loro _____

2. **conoscere** che io _____ che tu _____ che lui, lei _____

   (to know) che noi _____ che voi _____ che loro _____

3. **venire** che io _____ che tu _____ che lui, lei _____

   (to come) che noi _____ che voi _____ che loro _____

13. Practice

Write the verbs in the *imperfect subjunctive* in the person indicated.

Che io:

parlare   leggere   pulire

_____   _____   _____

Che tu:

comprare   vedere   finire

_____   _____   _____

Che lui:

andare   potere   sentire

_____   _____   _____

Che lei:

arrivare   correre   partire

_____   _____   _____

Che noi:

dimenticare   bere   dormire

_____   _____   _____

Che voi:

perdonare   scrivere   venire

_____   _____   _____

Che loro:

studiare   temere   capire

_____   _____   _____

14. Practice

Write the verbs in the *imperfect subjunctive* in the person indicated.

Pensavo che tu:

fare   vincere   capire

_____   _____   _____

Pensavo che lui:

lavorare   perdere   finire

_____   _____   _____

Pensavo che lei:

studiare   correggere   sentire

_____   _____   _____

Pensavo che noi:

cambiare   sapere   dormire

_____   _____   _____

Pensavo che voi:

sognare   accendere   costruire

_____   _____   _____

Pensavo che loro:

insegnare   spegnere   venire

_____   _____   _____

Speravo che tu:

parlare   vedere   finire

_____   _____   _____

Speravo che voi:

fare   leggere   pulire

_____   _____   _____

15. Practice

Rewrite in Italian, using the *imperfect subjunctive.* Sometimes an *infinitive* will be needed.

1. I wanted you (s.) to come   _____

2. I hoped you (s.) would come   _____

3. You thought you (s.) could study   _____

4. You (s.) thought he would study   _____

5. You (s.) thought we would come   _____

6. I hoped you (pl.) would come   _____

7. I believed he would write   _____

8. I thought we would go   _____

9. You (s.) hoped they would call   _____

10. They thought I would remain   _____

11. You all thought he would play   _____

12. I thought you (s.) would clean   _____

13. I did not know you (s.) would go   _____

14. You (s.) wanted me to cook   _____

15. She would like you (s.) to read   _____

16. It would be necessary for you (s.) to leave   _____

17. My father wanted me to work   _____

18. It was difficult for you (s.) to go   _____

19. I did not know you (s.) were so tall   _____

20. She wanted me to ask the doctor   _____

21. I wished to sleep all day long   _____

22. I wished she slept all day long   _____

23. He wanted us to go   _____

24. I hoped they invited me   _____

16. Practice

Change the verbs in parentheses to the *present subjunctive* or to the *imperfect subjunctive* as needed.

1. Spero che tu (parlare)   _____

2. Speravo che tu (parlare)   _____

3. Dubito che noi (venire)   _____

4. Dubitavo che noi (venire)   _____

5. Pensiamo che lui (essere)   _____

6. Pensavamo che lui (essere)   _____

7. È probabile che io (studiare)   _____

8. Era probabile che lui (studiare)   _____

9. È necessario che voi (studiare)   _____

10. Era necessario che voi (studiare)   _____

11. Credo di (venire)   _____

12. Credevo di (venire)   _____

13. Dubitiamo che lui (imparare)   _____

14. Dubitavamo che lui (imparare)   _____

15. Credo che tu (sognare)   _____

16. Credeva che tu (sognare)   _____

17. È possibile che loro (fare)   _____

18. Era possibile che loro (fare)   _____

19. Penso che voi (ricordare)   _____

21. Spera che lui (arrivare)   _____

22. Speravo che lui (arrivare)   _____

23. Voglio che tu (scrivere)   _____

24. Volevo che tu (scrivere)   _____

Chapter 8

Past Subjunctive

1. Use of the Past Subjunctive

The past subjunctive *(congiuntivo passato)* is used in a dependent *che* clause to express the speaker's feelings toward a recent past action when the verb in the main clause is in the present indicative. The present of *avere* or *essere* and the *past participle* of the verb are used.

Example: Credo che ***abbiano vinto*** la partita. I think that they won the game.

Note that the action in the *che* clause is in the past in relation to the action in the main clause, which is in the present tense.

2. Forms of the Past Subjunctive

The following chart shows the conjugations of ***trovare, vedere, partire*** in the past subjunctive.

	Trovare (To find)	**Credere** (To believe)	**Sentire** (To hear)
che io	abbia trovato	abbia creduto	abbia sentito
che tu	abbia trovato	abbia creduto	abbia sentito
che lui	abbia trovato	abbia creduto	abbia sentito
che lei	abbia trovato	abbia creduto	abbia sentito
che noi	abbiamo trovato	abbiamo creduto	abbiamo sentito
che voi	abbiate trovato	abbiate creduto	abbiate sentito
che loro	abbiano trovato	abbiano creduto	abbiano sentito

Conjugation of the past subjunctive using *essere*

	Partire (To leave, to depart)
che io	sia partito/a
che tu	sia partito/a
che lui	sia partito
che lei	sia partita
che noi	siamo partiti/e
che voi	siate partiti/e
che loro	siano partiti/e

3. Practice

Write the *past subjunctive* of the verbs in the person indicated.

Che io:

arrivare	vedere	finire
_____	_____	_____

Che tu:

parlare	leggere	capire
_____	_____	_____

Che lui:

ascoltare	scrivere	sentire
_____	_____	_____

Che lei:

piantare	scendere	salire
_____	_____	_____

Che noi:

studiare	vendere	sostituire
_____	_____	_____

Che voi:

cancellare	bere	venire
_____	_____	_____

Che loro:

guardare	mantenere	partire
_____	_____	_____

Che io:

non sperare	non aspettare	non ridere
_____	_____	_____

4. Practice

Complete the sentences with the *past subjunctive.*

1. È bene che Paolo (venire) _____

2. Speriamo che lui (parlare) _____

3. Loro sono contenti che noi (studiare) _____

4. Mi dispiace che tu (perdere) _____

5. Sono contento che noi (andare) _____

6. È giusto che lui (pagare) _____

7. È possibile che la polizia (arrestare) _____

8. Ci dispiace che tu non (trovare) _____

9. Ci dispiace che voi non (mangiare) _____

10. È bene che Maria (partire) _____

11. Sono sorpreso che lui (telefonare) _____

12. È sorpreso che voi (telefonare) _____

13. È possibile che lei non (studiare) _____

14. Spero che loro (venire) _____

15. Spero che voi (nuotare) _____

16. È giusto che io (ritornare) _____

17. È impossibile che lui (finire) _____

18. Siamo contenti che lui (capire) _____

19. Non credo che tu (trovare) _____

20. È possibile che Carlo (partire) _____

21. È necessario che tu (scrivere) _____

22. Siamo contenti che loro (studiare) _____

23. Sono sorpreso che tu (studiare) _____

24. Ci dispiace che lui non (telefonare) _____

5. Practice

Write the verbs in three forms of the *subjunctive: present, imperfect, past.*

Present	Imperfect	Past
1. Che io parlare		
2. Che tu sentire		
3. Che lui capire		
4. Che lei venire		
5. Che noi offrire		
6. Che voi prendere		
7. Che loro vedere		
8. Che io non pensare		
9. Che tu non leggere		
10. Che lui non pulire		
11. Che noi non stare		

Pluperfect Subjunctive

6. Use of the Pluperfect Subjunctive

The pluperfect subjunctive *(congiuntivo trapassato)* is used when the action of the verb in the dependent clause happened before the action of the verb in the main clause, which is in the past.

It is formed by the imperfect subjunctive of *essere* and *avere* plus the *past participle* of the verb.

Example:

Pres. Ind.	Perfect Subj.	Imp. Ind.	Pluperfect Subj.

Credo che Mario sia venuto.
I think that Mario came.

Credevo che Mario fosse venuto.
I thought that Mario had come.

7. Forms of the Pluperfect Subjunctive

The following chart shows the conjugations of the *pluperfect subjunctive* with *essere* and *avere*.

	Partire	**Capire**
che io	*fossi partito/a*	*avessi capito*
che tu	*fossi partito/a*	*avessi capito*
che lui/lei	*fosse partito/a*	*avesse capito*
che noi	*fossimo partiti/e*	*avessimo capito*
che voi	*foste partiti/e*	*aveste capito*
che loro	*fossero partiti/e*	*avessero capito*

8. Practice

Rewrite in English.

1. Che io fossi arrivato _____

2. Che tu avessi pensato _____

3. Che noi fossimo partiti _____

4. Che voi aveste parlato _____

5. Che loro fossero venuti _____

9. Practice

Rewrite the sentences, using the *imperfect subjunctive* in the main clause and the *pluperfect subjunctive* in the *che* clause.

1. Sembra che sappia tutto (lui) _____

2. È possibile che arrivi (lei) _____

3. Speriamo che entri (lei) _____

4. Penso che lui arrivi _____

5. Dubito che sappia (tu) _____

6. Sembra che capisca (lui) _____

7. È meglio che tu vada _____

8. È meglio che loro partano _____

9. Sembra che io sappia _____

10. Preferisco che voi andiate _____

11. Preferiamo che tu studi _____

12. Sono sicuro che Carlo arrivi _____

13. Preferisce che impariamo _____

14. Sono contento che tu venga _____

15. Siamo sicuri che partano _____

16. È probabile che tu arrivi _____

17. Penso che tu venga _____

18. Dubito che lui trovi lavoro _____

19. Credo che lei cerchi lavoro _____

20. È necessario che io legga _____

21. È bene che loro comprino _____

22. È necessario che vendano _____

23. Spero che Carlo venda _____

Se Clauses and the Subjunctive

10. Contrary-to-Fact

To express a **contrary-to-fact** statement in the present or the future, the **imperfect subjunctive** is used in the **se clause.** The conditional is normally used in the main clause to express a conclusion to the action.

> **Example:**   *Se potessi,* verrei.   If I could, I would come.

To express a contrary-to-fact statement in the past, the pluperfect subjunctive is used in the **se clause** and the past conditional is used in the main clause.

> **Example:**   *Se avessi saputo, sarei venuto.*   If I had known, I would have come.

11. Wishes

Se + the **imperfect subjunctive** is used in exclamations to express wishes that may never materialize.

> **Examples:**   *Se avessi* tanti soldi!   If only I had a lot of money!
> *Se potessi* parlare!   If only I could talk!

12. Practice

Use the verbs in parentheses in the correct tense of the subjunctive.

1. Capirei se tu (spiegare)   _____

2. Studieresti se (potere)   _____

3. Compreremmo se (avere) i soldi   _____

4. Scriverebbe se (sapere)   _____

5. Verrebbe se (guidare)   _____

6. Avrebbe capito se tu (spiegare)   _____

7. Avrebbe studiato se (potere)   _____

8. Avremmo comprato se (avere) soldi _____

9. Avrebbe scritto se (sapere)   _____

10. Sarebbe venuto se (guidare)   _____

11. Avresti comprato se lui (vendere) _____

12. Sarei andato se (sapere)   _____

Avresti parlato se tu (potere)   _____

Avreste capito se voi (studiare)   _____

_____

Reflexive Verbs

13. The Nature of Reflexive Verbs

A reflexive verb *(verbo riflessivo)* is one in which the object of the verb is the same person or thing as the subject. They are more common in Italian than in English.

Examples:	*Mi pettino.*	I comb my hair.
	Mi sveglio presto.	I wake up early.
	Carlo *si diverte.*	Carlo enjoys himself.

Some Italian verbs have both reflexive and nonreflexive forms.

Examples:	Noi *laviamo* tutti i giorni.	We wash every day.
	Noi *ci laviamo* tutti i giorni.	We wash ourselves every day.

Plural reflexive verbs used with the reflexive pronouns *ci, vi,* and *si* express a reciprocal meaning.

Example:	*Ci vediamo* ogni lunedì.	We see each other every Monday.
	Si scrivono spesso.	They write each other often.

Note: In Italian, the *reflexive* is often used where English uses an impersonal construction or the passive.

Examples:	Qui *si parla* italiano.	Here one speaks Italian.
	Come *si va* alla stazione?	How do you go to the station?
	Come *si fa* la pizza?	How do you make pizza?

14. Forms of Reflexive Verbs

In the present tense, the reflexive pronoun comes before the verb, but in the infinitive it is attached to the end, with the final *e* of the infinitive dropped.

Examples:	*Mi lavo* subito.	I wash myself right away.
	Vado a *lavarmi* subito.	I'm going to wash myself right away.

In the passato prossimo, reflexive verbs always use the auxiliary *essere* and a past participle that agrees with the subject.

Examples:	Giovanni *si è* addormentato.	Giovanni fell asleep.
	Carla *si è* addormentata.	Carla fell asleep.

Following is the conjugation of the present tense of *alzarsi*. The other tenses follow the same patterns of the regular verbs with the exception of the pronoun, which has to be placed in front of the verb.

Alzarsi			To get up
io	*mi*	*alzo*	I get up
tu	*ti*	*alzi*	you get up
lui	*si*	*alza*	he gets up
lei	*si*	*alza*	she gets up
noi	*ci*	*alziamo*	we get up
voi	*vi*	*alzate*	you get up
loro	*si*	*alzano*	they get up

15. List of Common Reflexive Verbs

Here is a list of some common reflexive verbs in Italian. They are not necessarily reflexive in English.

addormentarsi	to fall asleep
aiutarsi	to help one another
alzarsi	to get up
amarsi	to love each other
chiamarsi	to be called
divertirsi	to enjoy oneself, to have a good time
incontrarsi	to meet each other
innamorarsi	to fall in love
lavarsi	to wash oneself
mettersi	to put on (clothing)
mettersi a	to start, to begin
odiarsi	to hate one another
parlarsi	to speak to each other
prepararsi	to get ready
salutarsi	to greet one another
scriversi	to write each other
sentirsi	to feel
svegliarsi	to wake up
vedersi	to see each other
vestirsi	to get dressed

16. Practice

Write the verbs in the present indicative in the person indicated.

Io:

alzarsi

mettersi

sentirsi

_____

_____

_____

Tu:

addormentarsi

pettinarsi

domandarsi

_____

_____

_____

Lui:

lavarsi

pettinarsi

vestirsi

_____

_____

_____

Lei:

divertirsi

sposarsi

prepararsi

_____

_____

_____

Noi:

vestirsi

svegliarsi

aiutarsi

_____

_____

_____

Voi:

parlarsi

salutarsi

incontrarsi

_____

_____

_____

Loro:

divertirsi

sposarsi

prepararsi

_____

_____

_____

17. Practice

Rewrite in English.

1. Si sveglia (lui) _____

2. Lei si veste _____

3. Loro si preparano _____

4. Ci prepariamo _____

5. Vi salutate _____

6. Si parlano _____

7. Vi odiate _____

8. Si amano _____

9. Si mette a parlare _____

10. Si scrivono _____

11. Mi alzo _____

12. Ti lavi _____

13. Si lava (lui) _____

14. Carlo si veste _____

15. Ci incontriamo _____

16. Mi vesto _____

17. Si addormenta _____

18. Vi parlate _____

19. Si aiutano _____

20. Mi addormento _____

21. Si pettina (lui) _____

22. Si specchiano _____

23. Vi preparate _____

24. Si inginocchiano _____

18. Practice

Rewrite in Italian.

1. We wake up _____

2. I enjoy myself _____

3. They get up _____

4. They wake up _____

5. They greet each other _____

6. They get ready _____

7. He washes himself _____

8. She combs her hair _____

9. They meet each other _____

10. They enjoy themselves _____

11. She enjoys herself _____

12. He gets ready _____

13. You (pl.) get dressed _____

14. I get dressed _____

15. We help each other _____

16. We get up _____

17. We wake up _____

18. We love each other _____

19. We woke up _____

20. He got up _____

21. You (s.) washed yourself _____

22. She combed her hair _____

23. They hated each other _____

24. He enjoyed himself _____

Chapter 9

Progressive Tenses

1. Uses of the Progressive Tenses

In Italian, often the present and the imperfect tenses are used to express continuing actions, while in English the progressive tenses are generally used.

Examples:	*Mangiano.*	*They are eating.*
	Scrivo una lettera di affari.	*I am writing* a business letter.
	Parlavano.	*They were talking.*

In Italian, the progressive tense is used when one wants to emphasize that the action is going on at the time of speaking.

There are two progressive tenses: *present progressive* and *past progressive.*

Present Progressive:	Dove *stai andando?*	Where are you going?
Past Progressive:	Dove *stavi andando?*	Where were you going?

2. Forms of the Progressive

The progressive tenses are formed with the verb *stare* + the *gerund.* The gerund is formed by adding *-ando, -endo, -endo* forms to the infinitive stem of *-are, -ere,* and *-ire* verbs respectively.

Examples:	parlare	*parlando*
	tenere	*tenendo*
	sentire	*sentendo*

The present of *stare* is used for the *present progressive,* and the imperfect of *stare* is used for the *past progressive.*

Following are the complete conjugations of the *present progressive* and the *past progressive*.

Present Progressive

io	sto	parlando *(I am speaking)*
tu	stai	parlando
lui	sta	parlando
lei	sta	parlando
noi	stiamo	parlando
voi	state	parlando
loro	stanno	parlando

Past Progressive

io	stavo	parlando *(I was speaking)*
tu	stavi	parlando
lui	stava	parlando
lei	stava	parlando
noi	stavamo	parlando
voi	stavate	parlando
loro	stavano	parlando

Note: Reflexive pronouns may precede or follow *stare*.

Example: Lei *si sta pettinando.*   She is combing her hair.

or

Lei *sta pettinandosi.*   She is combing her hair.

3. Practice

Change the present tense into the *present progressive* and the imperfect to the *past progressive.*

A.

1.   Io parlo _____

2.   Tu ascolti _____

3.   Noi parliamo_____

4.   Lui guida _____

5.   Lei sente _____

6.   Noi studiamo _____

7.   Voi partite_____

8.   Tu leggi _____

9.   Lei parla _____

10.   Io gioco_____

11.   Tu parti _____

12.   Loro tornano_____

B.

1.   Tu andavi _____

2.   Tu ascoltavi _____

3.   Voi parlavate _____

4.   Io bevevo _____

5.   Voi vedevate_____

6.   Noi giocavamo_____

7.   Voi scrivevate_____

8.   Lui leggeva _____

9.   Tu prendevi _____

10.   Io bevevo _____

11.   Tu partivi _____

12.   Io tornavo _____

Modal Verbs

4. Common Modal Verbs

A *modal verb* is a special verb usually followed by an infinitive. The common modal verbs are:

dovere (must, to have to, should) expresses duty
potere (to be able to, can) expresses ability
volere (to want) expresses wants

Devo studiare. I must (have to) study.
Possono rimanere. They can stay.
Vogliamo pagare. We want to pay.

Note: All *modal verbs* are sometimes used without the infinitive, mainly in responses.

> Examples: *Puoi leggere* un po'? Can you read a little?
> No, non *posso.* No, I can't.

The modal verbs are conjugated with *avere* in the compound tenses when the infinitive following the modal verb is transitive, with *essere* if the infinitive is intransitive.

> Examples: Maria *ha dovuto* pagare. Mary had to pay.
> Maria *è dovuta andare* a pagare. Mary had to go to pay.

5. Forms of the Modal Verbs

	Dovere	Volere	Potere
Present:	devo	voglio	posso
	devi	vuoi	puoi
	deve	vuole	può
	dobbiamo	vogliamo	possiamo
	dovete	volete	potete
	devono	vogliono	possono
Future:	dovrò	vorrò	potrò
	dovrai	vorrai	potrai
	dovrà	vorrà	potrà
	dovremo	vorremo	potremo
	dovrete	vorrete	potrete
	dovranno	vorranno	potranno
Imperf.:	dovevo	volevo	potevo
	dovevi	volevi	potevi
	etc.	etc.	etc.

	Dovere	**Volere**	**Potere**
Passato ***Prossimo:***	ho (sono) dovuto hai (sei) dovuto etc.	ho (sono) voluto hai (sei) voluto etc.	ho (sono) potuto hai (sei) potuto etc.
Present ***Condit.:***	dovrei dovresti dovrebbe dovremmo dovreste dovrebbero	vorrei vorresti vorrebbe vorremmo vorreste vorrebbero	potrei potresti potrebbe potremmo potreste potrebbero
Past ***Condit.:***	avrei (sarei) dovuto avresti (saresti) dovuto etc.	avrei (sarei) voluto avresti (saresti) voluto etc.	avrei (sarei) potuto avresti (saresti) potuto etc.
Present ***Subjunct.:***	che io, tu, lui debba che noi dobbiamo che voi dobbiate che loro debbano	che io, tu, lui voglia che noi vogliamo che voi vogliate che loro vogliano	che io, tu, lui possa che noi possiamo che voi possiate che loro possano
Imperfect ***Subjunct.:***	dovessi dovessi dovesse dovessimo doveste dovessero	volessi volessi volesse volessimo voleste volessero	potessi potessi potesse potessimo poteste potessero
Past ***Subjunct.:***	avessi (fossi) dovuto avessi (fossi) dovuto avesse (fosse) dovuto etc.	avessi (fossi) voluto avessi (fossi) voluto avesse (fosse) voluto etc.	avessi (fossi) potuto avessi (fossi) potuto avesse (fosse) potuto etc.

Note: When ***dovere, volere, potere*** are conjugated with the verb ***essere,*** the past participle of the verb agrees in gender and number with the subject.

6. Practice

Rewrite in English.

Voglio andare

_____

Volevamo partire

_____

Vorrà portare

_____

Hanno voluto ascoltare

_____

Sono voluti venire

_____

Devo studiare

_____

Dovevamo arrivare

_____

Dovrà correre

_____

Hanno dovuto fare

_____

Sono dovuti andare

_____

Posso portare

_____

Potevamo sentire

_____

Potrà comprare

_____

Hanno potuto dire

_____

Sono potuti partire

_____

7. Practice

Rewrite in Italian.

I want to think

_____

You (s.) wanted to write

_____

We would like to come

_____

They have wanted to play

_____

I must go

_____

You (s.) had to see

_____

We should buy

_____

They have had to close

_____

I can sing

_____

You (s.) could sell (past)

_____

We could read (possibility)

_____

They could have cleaned

_____

The Passive Voice

In the *active voice* studied so far, the subject performs the action. In the *passive voice*, the subject receives the action.

Examples:	*Active Voice*	*Passive Voice*
	Maria *cucina* la cena.	La cena *è cucinato* da Maria.
	Mary *cooks* dinner.	Dinner *is cooked* by Mary.
	Maria *ha cucinato* la cena.	La cena *è stata cucinata* da Maria.
	Mary *cooked* dinner.	The dinner *was cooked* by Mary.

The *passive* in Italian is formed as in English, with the verb *essere* and the *past participle* of the verb needed. The past participle agrees with the subject in gender and number. The reflexive form is used instead of the *passive* in Italian when the person doing the action is not mentioned.

Examples:	La lettera *fu spedita*	The letter *was mailed*
	ieri da mio padre.	yesterday by my father.
	Si sono spedite le lettere ieri.	The letters *were mailed* yesterday.

8. Practice

Rewrite in English.

1. Quando è stato pagato il conto? _____

2. Da chi è stata scritta la Divina Commedia? _____

3. L'America è stata scoperta nel 1492. _____

4. Il ragazzo è stato svegliato. _____

5. La casa è finita. _____

9. Practice

Rewrite in Italian.

1. English is studied by many. _____

2. The game was played in the rain. _____

3. When was the dog found? _____

4. The house is cleaned by Paul. _____

5. The car was sold quickly. _____

Verbs That Follow Common Patterns

Many verbs in Italian are conjugated like other irregular verbs. By knowing the common verbs, you can conjugate many other verbs. Study these examples.

Dire

benedire	to bless
contraddire	to contradict
disdire	to retract
maledire	to curse
interdire	to forbid
predire	to predict

Fare

assuefarsi	to get accustomed
contraffare	to imitate
disfare	to undo
rifare	to redo
soddisfare	to satisfy
stupefare	to amaze

Porre

deporre	to put down
opporre	to oppose
proporre	to propose
supporre	to suppose

Prendere

contendere	to compete, to quarrel
distendere	to relax
estendere	to extend
fraintendere	to misunderstand
pretendere	to claim

Vedere

avvedersi	to become aware
intravedere	to glimpse
prevedere	to foresee
rivedere	to see again, to review

Venire

addivenire	to come to an agreement
divenire	to become
intervenire	to intervene
pervenire	to reach
prevenire	to anticipate

Cogliere

distogliere	to dissuade
raccogliere	to gather
togliere	to remove

Tenere

attenersi	to keep, to stick to
contenere	to contain
ottenere	to obtain

10. Practice

Write the verbs in the tense and person indicated.

Present

1. io (disdire) _____
2. tu (rifare) _____
3. voi (fraintendere) _____
4. loro (intervenire) _____
5. io (togliere) _____

6. lei (rifare) _____
7. loro (supporre) _____
8. lui (ottenere) _____
9. loro (interdire) _____
10. noi (rivedere) _____

Future

1. io (rifare) _____
2. loro (contendere) _____
3. lui (supporre) _____
4. noi (prevedere) _____
5. voi (rifare) _____

6. noi (opporre) _____
7. loro (ottenere) _____
8. io (predire) _____
9. lei (contraddire) _____
10. loro (intervenire) _____

Passato Remoto

1. loro (addivenire) _____
2. lui (prevedere) _____
3. loro (soddisfare) _____
4. noi (predire) _____
5. io (togliere) _____

6. voi (fraintendere) _____
7. lei (proporre) _____
8. loro (contraddire) _____
9. tu (prevenire) _____
10. loro (contraffare) _____

Passato Prossimo

1. io (stupefare) _____
2. tu (opporre) _____
3. noi (disdire) _____

4. loro (prevedere) _____
5. lei (ottenere) _____
6. tu (pretendere) _____

11. Practice

Rewrite in Italian. Use the *present, future,* or *passato remoto.*

1. They predicted _____

2. We'll relax _____

3. He becomes _____

4. We'll reach _____

5. She'll forbid _____

6. They supposed _____

7. They imitate _____

8. We anticipate _____

9. He'll foresee _____

10. You (s.) oppose _____

11. They'll satisfy _____

12. You (pl.) misunderstand _____

13. She gathered _____

14. You (s.) contradict _____

15. We competed _____

16. I'll remove _____

17. They'll amaze _____

18. He became aware _____

19. I redo _____

20. You relaxed _____

21. We suppose _____

22. I proposed _____

23. We dissuade _____

24. She gathers _____

25. I'll retract _____

26. We'll imitate _____

27. You (s.) oppose _____

28. You (pl.) became _____

29. We removed _____

30. She intervened _____

Chapter 10

General Review of Verbs

1. Present

Write the verbs in the *present indicative* in the person indicated.

Io:

parlare	vedere	sentire	capire
_____	_____	_____	_____

Tu:

camminare	scrivere	partire	finire
_____	_____	_____	_____

Lui:

lavorare	leggere	venire	pulire
_____	_____	_____	_____

Lei:

cucinare	temere	dire	uscire
_____	_____	_____	_____

Noi:

insegnare	volere	scoprire	offrire
_____	_____	_____	_____

Voi:

arrivare	vincere	avvenire	riuscire
_____	_____	_____	_____

Loro:

cambiare	perdere	morire	salire
_____	_____	_____	_____

2. Imperfect

Write the verbs in the *imperfect* in the person indicated.

io cominciare	tu parlare	lui arrivare	lei mangiare
_____	_____	_____	_____
lui perdere	lei vincere	noi dire	loro dare
_____	_____	_____	_____
noi venire	tu capire	lei finire	io salire
_____	_____	_____	_____
io parlare	tu diventare	lei comprare	noi passare
_____	_____	_____	_____
tu leggere	noi essere	voi scrivere	loro dovere
_____	_____	_____	_____
noi finire	voi dire	loro capire	tu finire
_____	_____	_____	_____
io chiudere	tu arrivare	lui partire	lei uscire
_____	_____	_____	_____
noi cambiare	voi scrivere	loro entrare	tu fuggire
_____	_____	_____	_____
io avere	tu dovere	noi andare	lui essere
_____	_____	_____	_____
noi potere	tu fare	lei uscire	loro volere
_____	_____	_____	_____
loro venire	lei dire	loro uscire	lei finire
_____	_____	_____	_____
io andare	loro capire	voi finire	tu partire
_____	_____	_____	_____

3. Future

A. Rewrite in English.

1. Mangerò _____

2. Sentirai _____

3. Salirà (lui) _____

4. Compreremo _____

5. Faremo _____

6. Studierò _____

7. Sentirò _____

8. Ascolterà _____

9. Partirete _____

10. Capirete _____

11. Farò _____

12. Vorrai _____

13. Dovrete _____

14. Vi alzerete _____

15. Guiderò _____

16. Voleremo _____

17. Fermerai _____

18. Saprò _____

19. Conoscerò _____

20. Arriveremo _____

21. Starò _____

22. Saremo _____

23. Leggerete _____

B. Rewrite in Italian.

1. I will go _____

2. You will sleep _____

3. He will eat _____

4. I will clean _____

5. She will walk _____

6. You (pl.) will call _____

7. I will listen _____

8. You (s.) will change _____

9. We will stay _____

10. They will enter _____

11. I will laugh _____

12. We will be able _____

13. I will see _____

14. You (pl.) will go _____

15. They will write _____

16. He will answer _____

17. I will have to _____

18. I will forget _____

19. She will clean _____

20. They will stay _____

21. I will do _____

22. She will close _____

23. They will drink _____

4. Passato Remoto and Passato Prossimo

Change the infinitive first into the *passato remoto,* then into the *passato prossimo.*

	Passato Remoto	**Passato Prossimo**
Io: andare	_____	_____
Tu: fare	_____	_____
Lui: venire	_____	_____
Lei: capire	_____	_____
Noi: vedere	_____	_____
Voi: pensare	_____	_____
Loro: sentire	_____	_____
Io: stare	_____	_____
Tu: chiedere	_____	_____
Lui: mandare	_____	_____
Lei: pensare	_____	_____

5. Trapassato Prossimo

A. Rewrite in English.

1. Avevo mangiato _____

2. Avevamo capito _____

3. Avevano dormito _____

4. Erano partiti _____

5. Ero andato_____

6. Eravamo stati _____

7. Avevamo parlato _____

8. Avevi studiato_____

9. Avevo capito_____

10. Avevo chiuso _____

11. Avevi sentito _____

12. Avevamo portato _____

13. Aveva perso (lui) _____

14. Avevate vinto _____

15. Avevo telefonato _____

16. Aveva finito (lei) _____

17. Ero stato _____

18. Erano saliti _____

19. Era scesa (lei)_____

20. Eravate partiti _____

21. Eravamo dispiaciute_____

22. Erano morti_____

23. Ero entrata _____

B. Rewrite in Italian, using the *trapassato prossimo.*

1. I had slept_____

2. He had entered _____

3. She had spoken _____

4. We had understood _____

5. You (pl.) had made _____

6. He had done_____

7. She had written _____

8. You (s.) had been _____

9. She had seen _____

10. We had come _____

11. They had returned _____

12. We had gone _____

13. I had eaten _____

14. You (s.) had written_____

15. They had cleaned_____

16. We had read_____

17. She had put _____

18. We had told _____

19. I had known _____

20. He had seen _____

21. I had wanted _____

22. You (pl.) had said _____

23. She was born _____

6. Present Conditional

Rewrite in Italian, using the *present conditional.*

1. I would like _____

2. I would read _____

3. You (pl.) would speak _____

4. She would listen _____

5. I would clean _____

6. They would write _____

7. We would think _____

8. I would answer _____

9. You (s.) would read _____

10. He would eat _____

11. She would sell _____

12. We would study _____

13. I would ski _____

14. They would travel _____

15. You (pl.) would drink _____

16. I would study _____

17. I should _____

18. I could _____

19. You (s.) would want _____

20. We would think _____

21. They would close _____

22. We would open _____

23. She would understand _____

7. Past Conditional

Rewrite in Italian, using the *past conditional.*

1. I would have liked _____

2. I would have been _____

3. She would have spoken _____

4. I would have listened _____

5. You (pl.) would have cleaned _____

6. They would have written _____

7. They would have thought _____

8. He would have read _____

9. We would have eaten _____

10. They would have arrived _____

11. I would have been _____

12. We would have stayed _____

13. You (s.) would have drunk _____

14. He would have studied _____

15. She would have gone _____

16. You (pl.) would have wanted _____

17. I would have closed _____

18. He would have opened _____

19. She would have thought _____

20. We would have understood _____

21. They would have traveled _____

22. You (s.) would have sung _____

23. They would have looked _____

24. We would have come _____

8. Present Subjunctive and Imperfect Subjunctive

Change the infinitive to the *present* and *imperfect subjunctive* in the person indicated.

		Present Subjunctive	**Imperfect Subjunctive**
1.	Che io mangiare	_____	_____
2.	Che tu vedere	_____	_____
3.	Che lui parlare	_____	_____
4.	Che lei sentire	_____	_____
5.	Che noi chiudere	_____	_____
6.	Che voi capire	_____	_____
7.	Che loro venire	_____	_____
8.	Che noi rispondere	_____	_____
9.	Che tu scrivere	_____	_____
10.	Che io imparare	_____	_____
11.	Che lui finire	_____	_____
12.	Che noi mangiare	_____	_____
13.	Che voi bere	_____	_____
14.	Che loro sapere	_____	_____
15.	Che tu telefonare	_____	_____
16.	Che lei prendere	_____	_____
17.	Che voi stare	_____	_____
18.	Che io stare	_____	_____
19.	Che voi dovere	_____	_____
20.	Che loro capire	_____	_____
21.	Che lei leggere	_____	_____
22.	Che tu mandare	_____	_____
23.	Che lui vendere	_____	_____

9. Past Subjunctive and Pluperfect Subjunctive

Change the following verbs to the *past subjunctive* and *pluperfect subjunctive.*

		Past Subjunctive	Pluperfect Subjunctive
1.	Che io venire	_____	_____
2.	Che lui parlare	_____	_____
3.	Che noi ascoltare	_____	_____
4.	Che lei fare	_____	_____
5.	Che voi finire	_____	_____
6.	Che voi andare	_____	_____
7.	Che loro chiudere	_____	_____
8.	Che tu aprire	_____	_____
9.	Che io potere	_____	_____
10.	Che lei dire	_____	_____
11.	Che noi finire	_____	_____
12.	Che tu capire	_____	_____
13.	Che io rispondere	_____	_____
14.	Che lei vedere	_____	_____
15.	Che voi parlare	_____	_____
16.	Che io vivere	_____	_____
17.	Che lei prendere	_____	_____
18.	Che loro viaggiare	_____	_____
19.	Che io ordinare	_____	_____
20.	Che voi insegnare	_____	_____
21.	Che tu bere	_____	_____
22.	Che lei aspettare	_____	_____
23.	Che tu ricevere	_____	_____

10. Present, Future, Imperfect, Passato Remoto

Change the following verbs to the tense and person indicated.

	Present	Future	Imperfect	Passato Remoto
Io fare				
Tu andare				
Lui mangiare				
Lei parlare				
Noi leggere				
Voi bere				
Loro vedere				
Io sentire				
Lui dare				
Voi stare				
Lei capire				
Loro finire				
Io rispondere				
Lui pulire				
Noi arrivare				
Voi salire				
Tu soffrire				
Lei offire				
Io imparare				
Lui vedere				
Lei cadere				
Lui morire				

11. Passato Prossimo and Trapassato Prossimo

Change the infinitive into the *passato prossimo* and *trapassato prossimo*.

		Passato Prossimo	Trapassato Prossimo
1.	Io capire	_____	_____
2.	Tu vedere	_____	_____
3.	Lei finire	_____	_____
4.	Lui leggere	_____	_____
5.	Noi ritornare	_____	_____
6.	Voi imparare	_____	_____
7.	Loro cenare	_____	_____
8.	Io pranzare	_____	_____
9.	Lei vendere	_____	_____
10.	Lui accendere	_____	_____
11.	Voi accettare	_____	_____
12.	Loro spegnere	_____	_____
13.	Io lavare	_____	_____
14.	Noi uscire	_____	_____
15.	Tu viaggiare	_____	_____
16.	Lui partire	_____	_____
17.	Lei guarire	_____	_____
18.	Voi arrivare	_____	_____
19.	Tu ascoltare	_____	_____
20.	Loro saltare	_____	_____
21.	Lui esaminare	_____	_____
22.	Noi dividere	_____	_____
23.	Lei stirare	_____	_____

12. Present Conditional and Past Conditional

Change the infinitive into *present conditional* and *past conditional*.

		Present Conditional	**Past Conditional**
1.	Io parlare	_____	_____
2.	Tu arrivare	_____	_____
3.	Lui cantare	_____	_____
4.	Lei lavare	_____	_____
5.	Lui lavorare	_____	_____
6.	Noi stare	_____	_____
7.	Voi andare	_____	_____
8.	Loro viaggiare	_____	_____
9.	Io vedere	_____	_____
10.	Tu potere	_____	_____
11.	Lui leggere	_____	_____
12.	Lei scrivere	_____	_____
13.	Noi correre	_____	_____
14.	Voi rispondere	_____	_____
15.	Loro cadere	_____	_____
16.	Io capire	_____	_____
17.	Tu finire	_____	_____
18.	Lui venire	_____	_____
19.	Noi sentire	_____	_____
20.	Voi offrire	_____	_____
21.	Loro pulire	_____	_____

13. Subjunctive Forms

Change the infinitive into the *four* different *tenses* of the *subjunctive* as indicated.

	Present	Imperfect	Past	Pluperfect
Io andare	_____	_____	_____	_____
Tu ritornare	_____	_____	_____	_____
Lui dare	_____	_____	_____	_____
Lei fare	_____	_____	_____	_____
Noi stare	_____	_____	_____	_____
Voi bere	_____	_____	_____	_____
Loro vedere	_____	_____	_____	_____
Noi fermare	_____	_____	_____	_____
Lui sentire	_____	_____	_____	_____
Lei dividere	_____	_____	_____	_____
Lui pagare	_____	_____	_____	_____
Tu vendere	_____	_____	_____	_____
Io dormire	_____	_____	_____	_____
Loro contare	_____	_____	_____	_____
Voi dire	_____	_____	_____	_____
Lei giocare	_____	_____	_____	_____
Lui saltare	_____	_____	_____	_____
Noi guardare	_____	_____	_____	_____
Tu salire	_____	_____	_____	_____
Voi leggere	_____	_____	_____	_____
Loro tirare	_____	_____	_____	_____
Noi pensare	_____	_____	_____	_____

Chapter 11

Idiomatic Expressions with *Avere* and *Fare*

1. Idioms with the Verb *Avere*

Here are some common idioms with **avere.**

Note: The infinitive **avere** is frequently abbreviated to **aver** before a consonant. This usage is followed in the idioms presented below.

1.	**avere (aver) . . . anni**	to be . . . years old
2.	**aver bisogno (di)**	to need
3.	**aver caldo**	to feel (be) warm
4.	**aver fame**	to be hungry
5.	**aver freddo**	to be cold
6.	**aver fretta**	to be in a hurry
7.	**avere l'impressione (di)**	to have the impression
8.	**avere intenzione (di)**	to have the intention
9.	**aver mal (di)**	to have an ache
10.	**aver paura (di)**	to be afraid
11.	**aver ragione (di)**	to be right
12.	**aver sete**	to be thirsty
13.	**aver sonno**	to be sleepy
14.	**aver torto (di)**	to be wrong
15.	**aver vergogna (di)**	to be ashamed (of)
16.	**aver voglia (di)**	to feel like doing

2. Practice

Rewrite in Italian, using idiomatic expressions with *avere.*

1. I need shoes _____

2. I am warm _____

3. You are cold _____

4. We are in a hurry _____

5. They have a headache _____

6. I am afraid _____

7. She is thirsty _____

8. He was sleepy _____

9. They were right _____

10. I was wrong _____

11. We are ashamed _____

12. I feel like eating _____

13. You (pl.) were hungry _____

14. They were in a hurry _____

15. I would be thirsty _____

16. They would need shoes _____

17. She would be right _____

18. We would be wrong _____

19. I would be afraid _____

20. He would have the intention _____

21. I have had a headache _____

22. They have been afraid _____

23. We have been afraid _____

3. Idioms with the Verb *Fare*

The verb *fare* is used in many idiomatic expressions.

Note: The infinitive of *fare* is frequently abbreviated to *far* before a consonant.

1.	**fare alla romana**	to go Dutch
2.	**fare bella, brutta figura**	to make a good, bad impression
3.	**fare attenzione**	to pay attention
4.	**fare benzina**	to get gas
5.	**fa caldo, freddo**	it is warm, cold
6.	**fare carriera**	to be successful
7.	**fare colazione**	to have breakfast
8.	**fare colpo su qualcuno**	to impress someone
9.	**fare compere**	to go shopping
10.	**fare esercizio**	to exercise
11.	**fare fotografie**	to take pictures
12.	**fare il bagno**	to take a bath
13.	**fare la conoscenza di**	to make the acquaintance
14.	**fare una crociera**	to take a cruise
15.	**fare la doccia**	to take a shower
16.	**fare lo jogging**	to jog
17.	**fare il pieno**	to fill up with gas
18.	**fare la spesa**	to get groceries
19.	**fare male**	to hurt, to ache
20.	**fare parte di**	to be part of
21.	**fare una passeggiata**	to take a walk
22.	**fare presto**	to hurry up
23.	**fare progresso**	to progress

24.	**fare quattro chiacchiere**	to chat
25.	**fare il campeggio**	to go camping
26.	**fare un complimento**	to pay a compliment
27.	**fare un discorso**	to make a speech
28.	**fare la predica**	to preach
29.	**fare una domanda**	to ask a question
30.	**fare un giro**	to take a tour
31.	**fare uno spuntino**	to have a snack
32.	**fare un viaggio**	to take a trip
33.	**fare un regalo**	to give a gift
34.	**fare visita**	to pay a visit
35.	**farsi male**	to get hurt
36.	**fare un favore (a)**	to do a favor
37.	**fare un piacere (a)**	to do a favor
38.	**far vedere a qualcuno**	to show someone

Weather Expressions

Che tempo fa?	How is the weather?
Fa bel tempo (cattivo).	The weather is good (bad).
Fa caldo (freddo).	It is warm (cold).

4. Practice

Rewrite in Italian, using idiomatic expressions with *fare.*

1. We go Dutch   _____
2. He pays attention   _____
3. I have breakfast   _____
4. We take a bath   _____
5. They have taken a cruise   _____
6. She goes shopping   _____
7. You (s.) got hurt   _____
8. I do a favor   _____
9. They take a walk   _____
10. I'll take pictures   _____
11. She took a trip   _____
12. You (pl.) ask a question   _____
13. He has a snack   _____
14. We hurry up   _____
15. It is warm   _____
16. We give a gift   _____
17. I pay a visit   _____
18. It was cold   _____
19. He preaches   _____
20. She'll make a speech   _____
21. They chat   _____
22. He made a bad impression   _____

Verbs and Expressions Followed by Prepositions

5. Verbs and Expressions Followed by the Preposition *a*

A. Before a Noun or Pronoun

assistere a	to attend	**fare vedere a**	to show
assomigliare a	to resemble	**fare visita a**	to visit
credere a	to believe in	**fare un regalo a**	to give a present to
dare noia a	to bother	**giocare a**	to play a game
dar da mangiare a	to feed	**interessarsi a**	to be interested in
dare fastidio a	to bother	**partecipare a**	to participate in
dare retta a	to listen to	**pensare a**	to think about
dare torto a	to blame	**raccomandarsi a**	to ask favors of
dare la caccia a	to chase	**ricordare a**	to remind
dare un calcio a	to kick	**rinunciare a**	to give up
dare un pugno a	to punch	**servire a**	to be good for
fare attenzione a	to pay attention	**stringere la mano a**	to shake hands with
fare bene (male)	to be good (bad)	**tenere a**	to care about
fare piacere a	to please		

B. Before an Infinitive

abituarsi a	to get used to	insegnare a	to teach
affrettarsi a	to hurry	invitare a	to invite to
aiutare a	to help	mandare a	to send
cominciare a	to begin	obbligare a	to oblige
continuare a	to continue	pensare a	to think about
convincere a	to convince	persuadere a	to convince
costringere a	to compel	preparare a	to prepare
decidersi a	to make up	provare a	to try one's mind
divertirsi a	to have a good time	rinunciare a	to give up
fare meglio a	to be better off	riprendere a	to resume
fare presto a	to do fast	riuscire a	to succeed
imparare a	to learn	sbrigarsi a	to hurry
incoraggiare a	to encourage	servire a	to be good for

a + verbs of movement:

andare a	to go
correre a	to run
fermarsi a	to stop
passare a	to stop by
stare a	to stay
tornare a	to return
venire a	to come

6. Verbs and Expressions Followed by the Preposition *di*

A. Before a Noun or Pronoun

accorgersi di	to notice, realize	**nutrirsi di**	to feed on
avere bisogno di	to need	**occuparsi di**	to plan
avere paura di	to be afraid	**pensare di**	to have an opinion about
dimenticarsi di	to forget	**preoccuparsi di**	to worry about
fidarsi di	to trust	**ricordarsi di**	to remember
innamorarsi di	to fall in love	**ridere di**	to laugh at
interessarsi di	to be interested in	**soffrire di**	to suffer from
lamentarsi di	to complain	**trattare di**	to deal with
meravigliarsi di	to be surprised	**vivere di**	to live on

B. Before an Infinitive

accettare di	to accept	**finire di**	to finish
ammettere di	to admit	**ordinare di**	to order
aspettare di	to wait for	**pensare di**	to plan
augurare di	to wish	**permettere di**	to permit
avere bisogno di	to need	**pregare di**	to beg
cercare di	to try	**proibire di**	to prohibit
chiedere di	to ask	**promettere di**	to promise
confessare di	to confess	**proporre di**	to propose
consigliare di	to advise	**ringraziare di**	to thank
contare di	to plan	**sapere di**	to know
credere di	to believe	**smettere di**	to stop
decidere di	to decide	**sperare di**	to hope
dimenticare di	to forget	**suggerire di**	to suggest
dubitare di	to doubt	**tentare di**	to attempt
fingere di	to pretend	**vietare di**	to avoid

7. Verbs Followed by the Preposition *Su*

contare su	to count on	**riflettere su**	to ponder on
giurare su	to swear on	**scommettere su**	to bet on

8. Verbs Followed Directly by the Infinitive

amare	to love	**piacere**	to like
desiderare	to wish	**potere**	to be able
dovere	to have to, must	**preferire**	to prefer
fare	to make	**sapere**	to know how
gradire	to appreciate	**volere**	to want
lasciare	to let, allow		

9. Impersonal Verbs

basta	it is enough	**pare**	it seems
bisogna	it is necessary		

Note: These verbs may be followed directly by an infinitive.

10. Practice

Rewrite in English.

1. Impariamo a sciare _____

2. Comincio a capire _____

3. Ho dimenticato di studiare _____

4. Penso di venire _____

5. Ha bisogno di studiare _____

6. Pensava a te _____

7. Staremo a casa _____

8. Torneranno a Roma _____

9. Ho paura di tutto _____

10. Aspettano di venire _____

11. Ho bisogno di te _____

12. Lei continua a mangiare _____

13. Insegnava a guidare _____

14. Sperate di vedere _____

15. Mi accorgo di essere in ritardo _____

16. Si innamora di tutti _____

17. Non mi fido di lui _____

18. Lei vive di amore _____

19. Smetti di parlare! _____

20. Contate su vostra sorella _____

21. Ha tentato di camminare _____

22. Finge di guardare nel libro _____

23. Ridiamo di lui _____

24. Ringraziano di tutto _____

11. Practice

Rewrite in Italian.

1. I go dancing _____

2. We go study _____

3. Have you (s.) been to Rome? _____

4. I believe in ghosts _____

5. They think about vacation _____

6. I will try to come _____

7. We are thinking of going _____

8. I'll teach you to swim _____

9. I finish working _____

10. She feels like eating chocolate _____

11. I begin to speak _____

12. He stops in Paris _____

13. We try to come _____

14. Call me before you leave _____

15. You (s.) continue to study _____

16. They promised to go _____

17. I promised to come _____

18. They need to think _____

19. You (pl.) hope to sleep _____

20. They feel like traveling _____

21. Stop (s.) talking! _____

22. They pay attention to the teacher _____

Answer Key

Chapter 1

Page 5, Practice 8

1. canto, canti, canta, cantiamo, cantate, cantano
2. provo, provi, prova, proviamo, provate, provano
3. lavoro, lavori, lavora, lavoriamo, lavorate, lavorano
4. ricordo, ricordi, ricorda, ricordiamo, ricordate, ricordano
5. viaggio, viaggi, viaggia, viaggiamo, viaggiate, viaggiano
6. volo, voli, vola, voliamo, volate, volano

Page 6, Practice 9

Io:	studio, insegno, viaggio, salto
Tu:	parli, mangi, trovi, balli
Lui, Lei:	impara, entra, lava, riposa
Noi:	compriamo, arriviamo, aiutiamo, tagliamo
Voi:	parlate, imparate, aspettate, pensate
Loro:	spiegano, insegnano, contano, camminano

Page 7, Practice 10

1. mangiamo, 2. impara, 3. comprano, 4. canto, 5. cammini, 6. parlate, 7. studiamo, 8. cambia, 9. pensate, 10. nuota, 11. gioco, 12. pranziamo, 13. viaggiate, 14. ballano, 15. lavora, 16. laviamo, 17. penso, 18. impariamo, 19. ascolto, 20. ama, 21. abitate, 22. pagano, 23. entri, 24. ispezioniamo, 25. pensa, 26. mandi

Page 8, Practice 11

1. we eat, 2. I learn, 3. they buy, 4. I sing, 5. you (s.) walk, 6. you (pl.) speak, 7. we study, 8. I change, 9. you (pl.) think, 10. I swim, 11. I play, 12. we have lunch, 13. you (pl.) travel, 14. they dance, 15. he/she works, 16. we wash, 17. I think, 18. we learn, 19. I listen, 20. he/she loves, 21. you (pl.) live, 22. they pay, 23. you (s.) enter, 24. we inspect, 25. he/she thinks, 26. you (s.) send

Page 9, Practice 12

1. mangio, 2. pensi, 3. imparano, 4. cantiamo, 5. mangiate, 6. lui studia, 7. lei insegna, 8. imparo, 9. lavori, 10. lavano, 11. lei entra, 12. riposiamo, 13. aspetti, 14. cantano, 15. ballo, 16. saltiamo, 17. viaggio, 18. lui trova, 19. arriviamo, 20. aspettate, 21. lei aiuta, 22. compro, 23. lei trova, 24. studiamo

Negative and Interrogative Forms

1. non mangio, 2. non lavori, 3. non ricordiamo, 4. non lavorano, 5. non entra, 6. io non riposo, 7 mangi?, 8. lavori?, 9. ricordiamo?, 10. lavorano?, 11. entra?, 12. riposo?

Page 10, Practice 13

1. we speak, 2. you (s.) jump, 3. he/she thinks, 4. you (pl.) sing, 5. I play, 6. we eat, 7. they learn, 8. you (s.) find, 9. we enter, 10. you (s.) work, 11. we teach, 12. you (pl.) wash, 13. I rest, 14. he/she looks, 15. we walk, 16. you (pl.) bring, 17. you (s.) dance, 18. they speak, 19. he/she travels, 20. we help, 21. I remember, 22. he/she forgets, 23. I don't eat, 24. they don't walk, 25. you (pl.) don't work, 26. do you (s.) work?

Page 12, Practice 15

1. do, dai, dà, diamo, date, danno
2. faccio, fai, fa, facciamo, fate, fanno
3. sto, stai, sta, stiamo, state, stanno
4. vado, vai, va, andiamo, andate, vanno

Chapter 2

Page 15, Practice 3

1. divido, dividi, divide, dividiamo, dividete, dividono
2. chiudo, chiudi, chiude, chiudiamo, chiudete, chiudono
3. metto, metti, mette, mettiamo, mettete, mettono
4. convinco, convinci, convince, convinciamo, convincete, convincono
5. spingo, spingi, spinge, spingiamo, spingete, spingono
6. perdo, perdi, perde, perdiamo, perdete, perdono

Page 16, Practice 4

Io: apprendo, attendo, chiedo, chiudo
Tu: cadi, confondi, dividi, cresci
Lui, Lei: decide, difende, discute, conclude
Noi: apprendiamo, attendiamo, insistiamo, esistiamo
Voi: cadete, ridete, rispondete, nascondete
Loro: perdono, piangono, insistono, promettono

Page 17, Practice 5

1. temo, 2. attendi, 3. cade, 4. chiediamo, 5. assisti, 6. chiude, 7. confondono, 8. conosci, 9. decidono, 10. difende, 11. discute, 12. decidiamo, 13. chiede, 14. godi, 15. concludo, 16. insiste, 17. mettiamo, 18. perde, 19. prometto, 20. promettiamo, 21. piangiamo, 22. rispondono, 23. vedo, 24. vede, 25. scrivo, 26. piango

Negative and Interrogative Forms

1. non assisto, 2. non attendi, 3. non chiediamo, 4. non dividono, 5. non chiude, 6. non piange, 7. assisti?, 8. attendi?, 9. chiedi?, 10. dividono?, 11. chiudi?, 12. piangi?

Page 18, Practice 6

1. we learn, 2. he/she fears, 3. we assume, 4. they attend, 5. I fall, 6. you (pl.) believe, 7. he/she asks, 8. they close, 9. you (s.) correct, 10. you (pl.) conclude, 11. they share, 12. they confuse, 13. you (s.) know, 14. they know, 15. you (pl.) cook, 16. he/she cooks, 17. I decide, 18. you (pl.) defend, 19. we discuss, 20. we include, 21. he/she insists, 22. you (pl.) lose, 23. they lose, 24. they cry, 25. he/she pretends, 26. you (s.) answer, 27. I see, 28. you (s.) win, 29. he/she knows, 30. they win, 31. you (pl.) laugh, 32. they break, 33. I don't stay, 34. they don't allow, 35. we don't read, 36. do you (pl.) read?, 37. do you (s.) read?, 38. do we see?, 39. does he/she write?, 40. do they fear?, 41. don't you (pl.) see?, 42. don't you (s.) read?, 43. don't they write?, 44. don't we write?

Page 20, Practice 8

1. devo, devi, deve, dobbiamo, dovete, devono
2. scelgo, scegli, sceglie, scegliamo, scegliete, scelgono
3. posso, puoi, può, possiamo, potete, possono
4. so, sai, sa, sapiamo, sapete, sanno
5. tengo, tieni, tiene, teniamo, tenete, tengono
6. voglio, vuoi, vuole, voliamo, volete, vogliono

Page 23, Practice 10

1. avverto, avverti, avverte, avvertiamo, avvertite, avvertono
2. bollo, bolli, bolle, bolliamo, bollite, bollono
3. sento, senti, sente, sentiamo, sentite, sentono
4. capisco, capisci, capisce, capiamo, capite, capiscono
5. preferisco, preferisci, preferisce, preferiamo, preferite, preferiscono

Page 24, Practice 11

Io:	apro, capisco, offro, finisco
Tu:	dormi, avverti, bolli, senti
Lui, Lei:	preferisce, parte, veste, spedisce
Noi:	serviamo, vestiamo, apriamo, capiamo
Voi:	avvertite, seguite, costruite, istruite
Loro:	sentono, inseguono, investono, partono

Page 25, Practice 12

1. preferisco, 2. acconsenti, 3. copre, 4. godiamo, 5. fuggono, 6. capisce, 7. segue, 8. menti, 9. sento, 10. soffriamo, 11. aprono, 12. finisce, 13. applaudi, 14. converte, 15. applaudo, 16. dorme, 17. inghiottisco, 18. partite, 19. servono, 20. dormo, 21. preferisce, 22. capisco, 23. preferiamo, 24. costruisco

Negative and Interrogative Forms

1. non finisco, 2. non capisce, 3. non istruiscono, 4. non senti, 5. non dormo, 6. non applaudiamo, 7. non partiamo, 8. non soffro, 9. costruiamo?, 10. sente?, 11. capiscono?, 12. sentono?, 13. dorme?, 14. acconsenti?, 15. finisce?, 16. partiamo?

Page 26, Practice 13

1. you (s.) agree, 2. they applaud, 3. he/she opens, 4. they open, 5. we announce, 6. he/she boils, 7. I understand, 8. you (pl.) consent, 9. they convert, 10. I cover, 11. he/she builds, 12. he/she offers, 13. we enjoy, 14. you (pl.) sleep, 15. they follow, 16. we finish, 17. he/she escapes, 18. you (s.) heal, 19. they guarantee, 20. you (s.) swallow, 21. they chase, 22. he/she instructs, 23. they prefer, 24. you (pl.) follow, 25. you (pl.) clean, 26. they punish, 27. he/she hits, 28. I serve, 29. he/she suffers, 30. I substitute, 31. we send, 32. they substitute, 33. we suggest, 34. they transfer

Negative and Interrogative Forms

1. we don't sleep, 2. he/she doesn't suffer, 3. we don't understand, 4. he/she doesn't instruct, 5. you (s.) don't open, 6. do you (s.) agree?, 7. do they leave?, 8. do you (s.) sleep?, 9. do you (s.) understand?, 10. do you (pl.) clean?

Page 28, Practice 15

1. vengo, vieni, viene, veniamo, venite, vengono
2. dico, dici, dice, diciamo, dite, dicono
3. esco, esci, esce, usiamo, uscite, escono

Page 28, Practice 16

1. dici, 2. escono, 3. veniamo, 4. muoiono, 5. salgo, 6. dice, 7. esco, 8. vengono, 9. salgono, 10. usciamo, 11. salite, 12. muore, 13. odi, 14. dicono, 15. udiamo, 16. dite

Chapter 3

Page 30, Practice 3

1. parla, 2. canta, 3. andate, 4. non andare, 5. andiamo, 6. non mangiate, 7. finiamo, 8. non giocate, 9. gioca, 10. guarda, 11. ascolta, 12. non partire, 13. partiamo, 14. giocate, 15. giochiamo, 16. esci, 17. non uscite, 18. gioca, 19. non giocare, 20. mangiate, 21. scrivi, 22. non scrivere, 23. scriviamo, 24. chiudi, 25. non chiudere, 26. chiudiamo, 27. dormi, 28. dormite, 29. bevi, 30. bevete, 31. leggi, 32. leggiamo, 33. non leggere, 34. non leggete

Page 31, Practice 4

1. speak (pl.), 2. sing, 3. don't sing, 4. listen, 5. listen (pl.), 6. let's go, 7. speak, 8. don't speak, 9. let's play, 10. don't play (pl.), 11. go out (pl.), 12. don't go out, 13. eat, 14. let's eat, 15. close, 16. ask (pl.), 17. think, 18. don't think (pl.), 19. suggest, 20. leave, 21. put (pl.), 22. don't put, 23. hope, 24. come in (pl.), 25. study, 26. don't study, 27. don't leave (pl.), 28. sing, 29. let's sing, 30. push, 31. don't push, 32. take (pl.)

Page 33, Practice 7

1. aspetti, 2. aspettino, 3. paghi, 4. paghino, 5. mangi, 6. rispondano, 7. finisca, 8. guardino, 9. venga, 10. mangino, 11. risponda, 12. finiscano, 13. vengano, 14. esca, 15. partino, 16. mi dica, 17. pensi, 18. escano, 19. cammini, 20. cantino, 21. leggano, 22. sorrida

Page 35, Practice 9

1. vedrò, vedrai, vedrà, vedremo, vedrete, vedranno
2. andrò, andrai, andrà, andremo, andrete, andranno
3. capirò, capirai, capirà, capiremo, capirete, capiranno
4. aiuterò, aiuterai, aiuterà, aiuteremo, aiuterete, aiuteranno

Page 36, Practice 10

Io:	parlerò, vedrò, pulirò
Tu:	viaggerai, permetterai, capirai
Lui, Lei:	troverà, saprà, sentirà
Noi:	guarderemo, berremo, finiremo
Voi:	lavorerete, avrete, partirete
Loro:	andranno, saranno, sentiranno

Page 37, Practice 11

1. I'll understand, 2. I'll work, 3. you'll (s.) read, 4. he/she'll sing, 5. you'll (pl.) hear, 6. you'll (s.) plant, 7. I'll listen, 8. you'll (pl.) plant, 9. we'll see, 10. they'll answer, 11. I'll pay, 12. we'll play, 13. you'll (s.) think, 14. you'll (pl.) see, 15. you'll (s.) hear, 16. I'll decide, 17. we'll cry, 18. he/she'll win, 19. you'll (pl.) discuss, 20. we'll go, 21. I'll study, 22. you'll (pl.) think, 23. you'll (s.) write, 24. I'll cook, 25. I'll finish, 26. we'll play, 27. we'll stay, 28. you'll (s.) do/make, 29. you'll (pl.) give, 30. you'll (s.) leave, 31. you'll (pl.) tell, 32. we'll sleep, 33. you'll (s.) chase, 34. we'll come, 35. I'll boil, 36. they'll applaud, 37. he/she'll open, 38. we'll climb

Negative Future Forms

1. I won't eat, 2. we won't go, 3. he/she won't do/make, 4. we won't sing, 5. he/she won't understand, 6. you (pl.) won't finish

Page 38, Practice 12

1. attenderò, 2. cadrà, 3. scriveremo, 4. penseranno, 5. capiremo, 6. chiuderò, 7. parlerai, 8. giocheremo, 9. viaggeranno, 10. metterò, 11. faremo, 12. troverà, 13. troveremo, 14. ascolterò, 15. impareremo, 16. mangerò, 17. andremo, 18. faranno, 19. starò, 20. comprerò, 21. verranno, 22. verrò, 23. guarderemo, 24. diremo, 25. dirà, 26. canteranno, 27. piangeremo, 28. pianterò, 29. usciremo, 30. saliranno, 31. andrete, 32. seguiremo, 33. insisterà, 34. vedrà, 35. risponderemo, 36. pagherò, 37. voteremo, 38. deciderò, 39. berremo, 40. sentiremo

Negative Future Forms

1. non mangerò, 2. non ascolterà, 3. non berremo, 4. non mangeranno

Chapter 4

Page 40, Practice 3

1. pensavo, pensavi, pensava, pensavamo, pensavate, pensavano
2. bevevo, bevevi, beveva, bevevamo, bevevate, bevevano
3. finivo, finivi, finiva, finivamo, finivate, finivano
4. abitavo, abitavi, abitava, abitavamo, abitavate, abitavano

Page 41, Practice 4

Io:	mangiavo, mettevo, sentivo
Tu:	cantavi, vedevi, finivi
Lui, Lei:	saltava, beveva, apriva
Noi:	votavamo, rispondevamo, costruivamo
Voi:	giocavate, comprendevate, applaudivate
Loro:	speravano, vendevano, preferivano

Page 42, Practice 5

A. 1. parlava, 2. cantavate, 3. abitava, 4. partivamo, 5. giocavate, 6. finivano, 7. camminavo, 8. perdevi, 9. comprendevate, 10. mangiavano, 11. costruivi, 12. istruivate, 13. lavorava, 14. ballava, 15. pensavano, 16. credevano, 17. lavavi, 18. scrivevamo, 19. correvo, 20. parlava

B. **Note:** The imperfect can be translated as **used to** or **was + verb ending in ing.** 1. we used to eat, 2. you (s.) used to study, 3. you (s.) used to drink, 4. you (s.) were playing, 5. he/she was listening, 6. you (pl.) used to understand, 7. they were writing, 8. I was asking, 9. you (pl.) were closing, 10. he/she used to listen, 11. we used to take, 12. I was learning, 13. we used to sell, 14. you (s.) used to sell, 15. you (s.) used to understand, 16. they were living, 17. he/she was instructing, 18. he/she used to see, 19. they were receiving, 20. I was teaching

Page 43, Practice 6

1. mangiavano, 2. pensavamo, 3. venivi, 4. credevo, 5. non pensavano, 6. imparavo, 7. credevano, 8. chiedevamo, 9. non volevi, 10. aspettava, 11. imparavano, 12. capivo, 13. potevi, 14. cantavamo, 15. volevano, 16. pensavo, 17. pensavamo, 18. voleva, 19. andava, 20. aspettavo, 21. speravo, 22. speravamo, 23. parlavo, 24. studiavi?, 25. parlavi?, 26. sperava, 27. pensavi, 28. lavoravamo, 29. volevano, 30. guardavamo, 31. guardavamo?, 32. viaggiava, 33. insegnavo, 34. mangiavano, 35. non capivo, 36. non potevo, 37. cantavano, 38. non volevano, 39. non pensavo, 40. pensavi, 41. voleva, 42. pulivo, 43. guardavamo, 44. non speravano, 45. sperava, 46. dubitavi

Page 44, Practice 9

1. mangiai, mangiasti, mangiò, mangiammo, mangiaste, mangiarono
2. potei, potesti, potè, potemmo, poteste, poterono
3. capii, capisti, capì, capimmo, capiste, capirono

Page 46, Practice 11

Io:	chiesi, conobbi, sentii
Tu:	comprasti, temesti, finisti
Carlo:	nacque, vide, volle
Maria:	capì, scrisse, venne
Noi:	facemmo, bevemmo, ridemmo
Voi:	scendeste, vinceste, metteste
Loro:	offrirono, partirono, fecero

Page 47, Practice 12

1. I came, 2. I laughed, 3. I drank, 4. he fell, 5. she asked, 6. we closed, 7. you (pl.) knew, 8. you (s.) said, 9. she decided, 10. we said, 11. you (pl.) must, 12. they said, 13. I lived, 14. they won, 15. you (s.) did/made, 16. she read, 17. we read, 18. you (s.) put, 19. you (pl.) were born, 20. I took, 21. we took, 22. you (s.) laughed, 23. they laughed, 24. she stayed, 25. you (s.) chose, 26. they wrote, 27. I chose, 28. you (s.) chose, 29. they wrote, 30. you (pl.) stayed, 31. you (s.) saw, 32. we saw, 33. you (pl.) won, 34. I saw, 35. they saw, 36. she lived, 37. he wanted, 38. we wanted, 39. they came, 40. you (s.) stayed

Page 48, Practice 13

1. I speak, 2. we eat, 3. they live, 4. do you (pl.) live?, 5. we drive, 6. I don't work, 7. we'll return, 8. they'll return, 9. I don't fly, 10. do you (pl.) fly?, 11. they'll arrive, 12. I'll arrive, 13. you won't (pl.) arrive, 14. I ask, 15. I wasn't asking, 16. they close, 17. do you (s.) close?, 18. I think, 19. you'll (s.) think, 20. we rest, 21. they rest, 22. you (s.) don't rest, 23. I spoke, 24. we thought, 25. do you (s.) rest?, 26. eat!, 27. look (pl.)!, 28. speak!, 29. learn!, 30. don't look!, 31. don't sleep!, 32. listen (formal)!, 33. do you (s.) promise?, 34. I'll answer, 35. we'll write, 36. I used to read, 37. you (s.) used to speak, 38. you (pl.) wanted, 39. they used to cry, 40. you (s.) used to insist, 41. you (s.) used to drink, 42. drink!, 43. drink! (pl.), 44. don't drink!, 45. you (s.) come, 46. do you (s.) come?, 47. he/she read, 48. you (pl.) heard

Page 49, Practice 14

1. abitano, 2. aprivo, 3. lavorarono, 4. saliamo, 5. capisco, 6. mangiarono, 7. mangiammo, 8. lavora, 9. studiano, 10. tengo, 11. scrivo, 12. scrivevi, 13. scriverò, 14. viaggi, 15. viaggiavi, 16. viaggeranno, 17. parto, 18. parte, 19. partiremo, 20. partiva, 21. imparava, 22. imparavamo, 23. pensavano, 24. vivrò, 25. apriremo, 26. mangia!, 27. lavora!, 28. mangerà, 29. lavorerà, 30. studia!, 31. studiate!, 32. bevi!, 33. bevete!, 34. promettevamo, 35. volevo, 36. deve, 37. rispondi!, 38. scriva!, 39. aspetti!, 40. dissi, 41. aspetteremo, 42. discuto, 43. vedevamo, 44. sanno, 45. capiamo, 46. pensavo

Chapter 5

Page 56, Practice 7

1. ho mangiato, hai mangiato, ha mangiato, abbiamo mangiato, avete mangiato, hanno mangiato
2. ho scritto, hai scritto, ha scritto, abbiamo scritto, avete scritto, hanno scritto
3. sono venuto/a, sei venuto/a, è venuto/a, siamo venuti/e, siete venuti/e, sono venuti/e
4. sono andato/a, sei andato/a, è andato/a, siamo andati/e, siete andati/e, sono andati/e

Page 57, Practice 8

Io:	ho mangiato	ho visto	ho sentito
Tu:	hai parlato	hai scritto	hai capito
Lui:	ha viaggiato	ha potuto	ha finito
Lei:	ha camminato	ha voluto	è venuta
Noi:	abbiamo lodato	abbiamo spinto	siamo saliti/e
Voi:	siete stati/e	avete riso	avete aperto
Loro:	hanno dato	sono rimasti/e	hanno nutrito
Carlo:	ha fatto	è nato	ha offerto
Maria:	è andata	ha nascosto	ha pulito
Io e Giovanni:	abbiamo aspettato	abbiamo venduto	siamo partiti
Tu e Pietro:	avete imparato	avete chiuso	siete usciti
Giovanni e Paolo:	hanno fermato	hanno vissuto	hanno finito

Page 58, Practice 9

Io:	non sono stato/a	non ho avuto	non ho potuto
Tu:	non hai voluto	non hai dovuto	non hai capito
Lui:	non ha fatto	non ha dato	non è stato
Noi:	non siamo andati/e	non siamo arrivati/e	non siamo partiti/e

Page 59, Practice 10

1. ha parlato, 2. siamo stati/e, 3. è stata, 4. avete letto, 5. hanno sentito, 6. ho dormito, 7. hai perso, 8. è andata, 9. ha deciso, 10. abbiamo comprato, 11. avete vissuto, 12. hanno bevuto, 13. ha parlato, 14. ha aperto, 15. ha aperto, 16. avete imparato, 17. abbiamo temuto, 18. ho mangiato, 19. hai ricevuto, 20. ha lavorato, 21. abbiamo viaggiato, 22. hanno potuto, 23. avete insegnato, 24. abbiamo sciato, 25. abbiamo corso, 26. ho guardato, 27. hai guarito, 28. avete risposto, 29. sono arrivati/e, 39. abbiamo tenuto, 31. ha venduto, 32. hanno vissuto, 33. ho abitato, 34. abbiamo gettato

Page 59, Practice 11

1. non ha mangiato, 2. non ha comprato, 3. non hai parlato, 4. non ho studiato, 5. non hanno dovuto, 6. non abbiamo cantato, 7. non hanno visto, 8. non avete sentito, 9. non hai scritto, 10. non abbiamo voluto

Page 60, Practice 12

1. abbiamo risposto, 2. hanno comprato, 3. abbiamo imparato, 4. ha comprato, 5. ho chiesto, 6. hai risposto, 7. abbiamo lasciato, 8. ho bevuto, 9. non ho bevuto, 10. hanno insegnato, 11. ho letto, 12. hai scritto, 13. hanno lavorato, 14. ha dormito, 15. ha lavorato, 16. abbiamo studiato, 17. non ha sciato, 18. non è andata, 19. è nata, 20. hanno venduto, 21. non ho ascoltato, 22. non ho sentito, 23. non ho chiesto, 24. non hai risposto, 25. ho ricevuto, 26. ho imparato, 27. hanno capito, 28. ha viaggiato, 29. non abbiamo viaggiato, 30. hanno pulito, 31. abbiamo pensato, 32. non hanno pensato, 33. ho pulito, 34. hai pagato, 35. non hai pagato, 36. abbiamo mangiato, 37. sono arrivato/a, 38. sono stati/e

Page 61, Practice 15

1. avevo guardato, avevi guardato, aveva guardato, avevamo guardato, avevate guardato, avevano guardato
2. avevo visto, avevi visto, aveva visto, avevamo visto, avevate visto, avevano visto
3. ero partito/a, eri partito/a, era partito/a, eravamo partiti/e, eravate partiti/e, erano partiti/e

Page 62, Practice 16

Io:	avevo mangiato	avevo visto	avevo sentito
Tu:	avevi parlato	avevi creduto	avevi pulito
Lui, Lei:	aveva visitato	aveva scritto	aveva finito
Noi:	eravamo arrivati/e	avevamo bevuto	avevamo capito
Voi:	avevate comprato	avevate letto	eravate venuti/e
Loro:	avevano dato	avevano potuto	avevano aperto
Carlo:	aveva giocato	aveva spinto	aveva costruito
Carlo e Maria:	avevano viaggiato	avevano venduto	erano partiti

Page 63, Practice 17

1. avevo capito, 2. eri andato/a, 3. aveva studiato, 4. aveva bevuto, 5. avevamo finito, 6. avevate dormito, 7. avevano comprato, 8. avevo lavorato, 9. avevi pensato, 10. aveva giocato, 11. avevamo viaggiato, 12. avevate pulito, 13. avevano guardato, 14. ero stato/a, 15. eri arrivato/a, 16. era partito, 17. era andata, 18. avevamo letto, 19. avevate scritto, 20. avevamo finito, 21. avevo vinto, 22. aveva perso, 23. era andata, 24. avevamo ascoltato

Page 64, Practice 18

1. ho mangiato, 2. avevi mangiato, 3. è andata, 4. era venuto, 5. abbiamo finito, 6. avevamo finito, 7. avete visto, 8. avevate guardato, 9. hanno letto, 10. avevano letto, 11. ho giocato, 12. avevo dormito, 13. ha mangiato, 14. avevamo sciato, 15. non abbiamo letto, 16. non avevamo pensato, 17. non hanno vinto, 18. non avevamo promesso, 19. non ho scelto, 20. non è venuto, 21. non era partita, 22. abbiamo vissuto, 23. non abbiamo vissuto, 24. avevamo vissuto

Chapter 6

Page 66, Practice 3

1. andrei, andresti, andrebbe, andremmo, andreste, andrebbero
2. dovrei, dovresti, dovrebbe, dovremmo, dovreste, dovrebbero
3. verrei, verresti, verrebbe, verremmo, verreste, verrebbero

Io:	canterei	potrei	capirei
Tu:	balleresti	vedresti	dormiresti
Lui, Lei:	nuoterebbe	berrebbe	sentirebbe
Noi:	ordineremmo	leggeremmo	finiremmo
Voi:	viaggereste	dovreste	partireste
Loro:	domanderebbero	vorrebbero	verrebbero
Giovanna:	ascolterebbe	avrebbe	direbbe
Io e Carlo:	parleremmo	vedremmo	colpiremmo
Tu e Giovanna:	desiderereste	vincereste	ubbidireste
Giovanna e Carlo:	organizzerebbero	prometterebbero	offrirebbero

Page 68, Practice 5

Io:	non parlerei	non vedrei	non sentirei
Tu:	non viaggeresti	non scriveresti	non puliresti
Paolo:	non mangerebbe	non potrebbe	non capirebbe
Io e Carlo:	non studieremmo	non leggeremmo	non finiremmo
Tu e Paolo:	non arrivereste	non vorreste	non partireste

Page 69, Practice 6

1. I would buy, 2. you (s.) would see, 3. I would understand, 4. we wouldn't eat, 5. you (pl.) would come, 6. they would hear, 7. I would study, 8. I wouldn't study, 9. you (s.) would travel, 10. he/she would understand, 11. Carla would arrive, 12. we would be, 13. they would write, 14. I would sleep, 15. you (s.) wouldn't read, 16. Paolo wouldn't leave, 17. we would make/do, 18. you (pl.) would not play, 19. you (pl.) would be, 20. they would listen, 21. I would come, 22. I wouldn't come, 23. you (s.) would stay, 24. Carlo would understand, 25. Maria would cook, 26. we would play, 27. we would want, 28. we wouldn't want, 29. you and Paolo would do/make, 30. I wouldn't do/make, 31. we would go, 32. you (pl.) would bring, 33. Carla couldn't bring, 34. they should, 35. I would invite, 36. they would come

Interrogative Forms

1. would you (s.) come?, 2. would they sing?, 3. would he/she understand?, 4. would you (pl.) give?, 5. would he/she speak?, 6. would you (s.) listen?, 7. would we make/do?, 8. would you (s.) cook?

Page 70, Practice 7

1. penserei, 2. berrei, 3. potresti, 4. farebbe, 5. non farebbe, 6. scriverebbe, 7. lavorerei, 8. berrebbero, 9. pulirei, 10. farebbe, 11. laverebbero, 12. guarderei, 13. vedrebbero, 14. penseremmo, 15. laverei, 16. capiresti, 17. non andrebbero, 18. vedreste, 19. non prenderei, 20. saprei, 21. andresti, 22. non potresti, 23. penserebbe, 24. scriveremmo, 25. leggerebbero, 26. dormirei, 27. non potrebbero, 28. mangeremmo, 29. berrei, 30. viaggereste, 31. ritornerebbe, 32. arriverebbe, 33. partirebbero, 34. non arriverei, 35. non pianterebbe, 36. vincerebbe, 37. mangerebbero, 38. nuoteremmo, 39. sciereste, 40. guarderemmo

Page 70, Practice 8

1. dovrei andare, 2. dovresti scrivere, 3. dovrebbero studiare, 4. dovremmo venire, 5. dovrebbe cucinare, 6. dovrebbe leggere

Page 71, Practice 11

1. avrei parlato, avresti parlato, avrebbe parlato, avremmo parlato, avreste parlato, avrebbero parlato
2. avrei visto, avresti visto, avrebbe visto, avremmo visto, avreste visto, avrebbero visto
3. sarei venuto/a, saresti venuto/a, sarebbe venuto/a, saremmo venuti/e, sareste venuti/e, sarebbero venuti/e

Page 72, Practice 12

Io:	sarei andato/a	sarei ritornato/a	sarei partito/a
Tu:	avresti parlato	avresti venduto	avresti capito
Lui, Lei:	sarebbe arrivato/a	avrebbe scritto	avrebbe dormito
Noi:	avremmo informato	avremmo letto	avremmo preferito
Voi:	avreste aspettato	avreste dovuto	avreste finito
Loro:	avrebbero abitato	avrebbero bevuto	sarebbero usciti/e
Carlo:	avrebbe invitato	avrebbe voluto	avrebbe sentito

Page 73, Practice 13

1. I would have waited, 2. you (s.) would talk, 3. he/she would have eaten, 4. they would understand, 5. you (pl.) would write, 6. you (pl.) would have written, 7. they would answer, 8. he/she would not have answered, 9. I would hear, 10. I would have heard, 11. we would have signed, 12. I would invite, 13. you (pl.) would go out, 14. we would finish, 15. they would have finished, 16. you (pl.) would buy, 17. he would buy, 18. you (s.) would find, 19. I would have looked, 20. he/she would answer, 21. he/she would have answered, 22. you (pl.) would have written, 23. I would know, 24. he/she would have known

Page 74, Practice 14

1. andrei, 2. avresti preso, 3. avremmo ballato, 4. sarebbero venuti/e, 5. saprebbe, 6. aspetteremmo, 7. avremmo cominciato, 8. scriverebbe, 9. avrebbe risposto, 10. parlerebbero, 11. sarebbero dovuti/e venire, 12. avrei dovuto parlare, 13. dovrebbe aspettare, 14. avrebbe dovuto aspettare, 15. capiremmo, 16. avrebbero capito, 17. avrebbe scritto, 18. avresti risposto, 19. avresti dovuto rispondere, 20. viaggerebbero, 21. sarei ritornato, 22. sarebbe partito, 23. arriverebbe, 24. partiremmo

Chapter 7

Page 78, Practice 4

1. domandi, domandi, domandi, domandiamo, domandiate, domandino
2. veda, veda, veda, vediamo, vediate, vedano
3. senta, senta, senta, sentiamo, sentiate, sentano
4. capisca, capisca, capisca, capiamo, capiate, capiscano
5. giochi, giochi, giochi, giochiamo, giochiate, giochino
6. paghi, paghi, paghi, paghiamo, paghiate, paghino

Page 79, Practice 5

Che io:	domandi	decida	senta
Che tu:	compri	veda	finisca
Che lui:	prepari	legga	capisca
Che lei:	aspetti	comprenda	pulisca
Che noi:	arriviamo	accendiamo	diciamo
Che voi:	visitiate	beviate	partiate
Che loro:	lavorino	chiudano	capiscano

Page 80, Practice 6

Io voglio che tu:	mangi	legga	parta
Io voglio che lui:	parli	perda	offra
Io voglio che lei:	stia	discuta	apra
Io spero che noi:	impariamo	sorridiamo	capiamo
Io desidero che voi:	facciate	vediate	ridiate
Io penso che loro:	desiderino	debbano	ubbidiscano
Io voglio:	visitare	vincere	capire
Loro vogliono:	visitare	arrivare	partire

Page 81, Practice 7

1. legga, 2. studino, 3. comprino, 4. capisca, 5. venga, 6. arrivino, 7. finisca, 8. venga, 9. possa, 10. legga, 11. veniamo, 12. pensiate, 13. sapere, 14. ritorni, 15. sappia, 16. vada, 17. vinca, 18. perda, 19. pensino, 20. controlli, 21. possano, 22. sapere, 23. puliscano, 24. comprare

Page 82, Practice 8

1. che io vada, 2. che lui senta, 3. che noi mangiamo, 4. che loro parlino, 5. che voi sentiate, 6. che tu beva, 7. che lei parta, 8. che lui capisca, 9. che noi lavoriamo, 10. che voi sentiate, 11. che voi ascoltiate, 12. che loro leggano, 13. che voi non ascoltiate, 14. che voi andiate, 15. che io parta, 16. che lui arrivi, 17. che piova, 18. che io sappia, 19. che tu conosca, 20. che tu possa, 21. che voi non leggiate, 22. che voi compriate, 23. che voi vendiate, 24. che voi capiate

Page 83, Practice 9

1. vada, 2. partire, 3. arrivi, 4. pensi, 5. visiti, 6. andare, 7. capisca, 8. comprare, 9. veda, 10. possa, 11. vogliamo, 12. legga, 13. finire, 14. paghi, 15. ascolti, 16. compri, 17. vendiamo, 18. scriva, 19. guardino, 20. studi, 21. parta, 22. rimaniamo, 23. perdiate, 24. rimanga

Page 85, Practice 12

1. che io ascoltassi, che tu ascoltassi, che lui ascoltasse, che lei ascoltasse, che noi ascoltassimo, che voi ascoltaste, che loro ascoltassero
2. che io conoscessi, che tu conoscessi, che lui conoscesse, che lei conoscesse, che noi conoscessimo, che voi conosceste, che loro conoscessero
3. che io venissi, che tu venissi, che lui venisse, che lei venisse, che noi venissimo, che voi veniste, che loro venissero

Page 86, Practice 13

Che io:	parlassi	leggessi	pulissi
Che tu:	comprassi	vedessi	finissi
Che lui:	andasse	potesse	sentisse
Che lei:	arrivasse	corresse	partisse
Che noi:	dimenticassimo	bevessimo	dormissimo
Che voi:	perdonaste	scriveste	veniste
Che loro:	studiassero	temessero	capissero

Page 87, Practice 14

Pensavo che tu:	facessi	vincessi	capissi
Pensavo che lui:	lavorasse	perdesse	finisse
Pensavo che lei:	studiasse	correggesse	sentisse
Pensavo che noi:	cambiassimo	sapessimo	dormissimo
Pensavo che voi:	sognaste	accendeste	costruiste
Pensavo che loro:	insegnassero	spegnessero	venissero
Speravo che tu:	parlassi	vedessi	finissi
Speravo che voi:	faceste	leggeste	puliste

Page 88, Practice 15

1. volevo che tu venissi, 2. speravo che tu venissi, 3. pensavi di poter studiare, 4. pensavi che lui studiasse, 5. pensavi che venissimo, 6. speravo che tu veniste, 7. credevo che scrivesse, 8. pensavo che andassimo, 9. speravi che chiamassero, 10. pensavano che rimanessi, 11. tutti voi pensavate che giocasse, 12. pensavo che tu pulissi, 13. non sapevo che tu andassi, 14. volevi che io cucinassi, 15. vorrebbe che tu leggessi, 16. sarebbe necessario che tu partissi, 17. mio padre voleva che io lavorassi, 18. era difficile che tu andassi, 19. non sapevo che tu fossi così alto/a, 20. voleva che chiedessi al dottore, 21. volevo dormire tutto il giorno, 22. volevo che dormisse tutto il giorno, 23. voleva che andassimo, 24. speravo che mi invitassero

Page 89, Practice 16

1. parli, 2. parlassi, 3. veniamo, 4. venissimo, 5. sia, 6. fosse, 7. studi, 8. studiasse, 9. studiate, 10. studiaste, 11. venire, 12. venire, 13. impari, 14. imparasse, 15. sogni, 16. sognassi, 17. facciano, 18. facessero, 19. ricordiate, 20. ricordasse, 21. arrivi, 22. arrivasse, 23. scriva, 24. scrivessi

Chapter 8

Page 91, Practice 3

Che io:	sia arrivato/a	abbia visto	abbia finito
Che tu:	abbia parlato	abbia letto	abbia capito
Che lui:	abbia ascoltato	abbia scritto	abbia sentito
Che lei:	abbia piantato	sia scesa	sia salita
Che noi:	abbiamo studiato	abbiamo venduto	abbiamo sostituito
Che voi:	abbiate cancellato	abbiate bevuto	siate venuti/e
Che loro:	abbiano guardato	abbiano mantenuto	siano partiti/e
Che io:	non abbia sperato	non abbia aspettato	non abbia riso

Page 92, Practice 4

1. sia venuto, 2. abbia parlato, 3. abbiamo studiato, 4. abbia perso, 5. siamo andati/e, 6. abbia pagato, 7. abbia arrestato, 8. abbia trovato, 9. abbiate mangiato, 10. sia partita, 11. abbia telefonato, 12. abbiate telefonato, 13. abbia studiato, 14. siano venuti/e, 15. abbiate nuotato, 16. sia ritornato/a, 17. abbia finito, 18. abbia capito, 19. abbia trovato, 20. sia partito, 21. abbia scritto, 22. siano venuti/e, 23. abbia studiato, 24. abbia telefonato

Page 93, Practice 5

1. parli	parlassi	abbia parlato
2. senta	sentissi	abbia sentito
3. capisca	capisse	abbia capito
4. venga	venisse	sia venuta
5. offriamo	offrissimo	abbiamo offerto
6. prendiate	prendeste	aveste preso
7. vedano	vedessero	abbiano visto
8. pensi	pensassi	abbia pensato
9. legga	leggessi	abbia letto
10. pulisca	pulisse	abbia pulito
11. stiamo	stessimo	siamo stati

Page 94, Practice 8

1. That I had arrived
2. That you (s.) had thought
3. That we had left
4. That you (pl.) had spoken
5. That they had come

Page 95, Practice 9

1. Sembrava che avesse saputo tutto, 2. era possibile che fosse arrivata, 3. speravamo che fosse entrata, 4. pensavo che fosse arrivato, 5. dubitavo che avessi saputo, 6. sembrava che avesse capito, 7. era meglio che fossi andato/a, 8. era meglio che fossero partiti/e, 9. sembrava che io avessi saputo, 10. preferivo che foste andati/e, 11. preferivamo che tu avessi studiato, 12. ero sicuro che Carlo fosse arrivato, 13. preferiva che avessimo imparato, 14. ero contento che tu fossi venuto/a, 15. eravamo sicuri che fossero partiti/e, 16. era probabile che fossi arrivato/a, 17. pensavo che tu fossi venuto/a, 18. dubitavo che avesse trovato lavoro, 19. credevo che avesse cercato lavoro, 20. era necessario che io avessi letto, 21. era bene che avessero comprato, 22. era necessario che avessero venduto, 23. speravo che Carlo avesse venduto

1. spiegassi, 2 potessi, 3. avessimo, 4. sapesse, 5. guidasse, 6. avessi spiegato, 7. avesse potuto, 8. avessimo avuto, 9. avesse saputo, 10. avesse guidato, 11. avesse venduto, 12. avessi saputo, 13. avessi potuto, 14. aveste studiato

Page 99, Practice 16

Io:	mi alzo	mi metto	mi sento
Tu:	ti addormenti	ti pettini	ti domandi
Lui:	si lava	si pettina	si veste
Lei:	si diverte	si sposa	si prepara
Noi:	ci vestiamo	ci svegliamo	ci aiutiamo
Voi:	vi parlate	vi salutate	vi incontrate
Loro:	si divertono	si sposano	si preparano

Page 100, Practice 17

1. he wakes up, 2. she gets dressed, 3. they get ready, 4. we get ready, 5. you (pl.) greet each other, 6. they talk to each other, 7. you (pl.) hate each other, 8. they love each other, 9. he/she begins to talk, 10. they write each other, 11. I get up, 12. you wash yourself, 13. he washes himself, 14. Carlo gets dressed, 15. we meet each other, 16. I get dressed, 17. he/she falls asleep, 18. you (pl.) talk to each other, 19. they help each other, 20. I fall asleep, 21. he combs his hair, 22. they look at themselves in the mirror, 23. you (pl.) get ready, 24. they kneel

Page 101, Practice 18

1. ci svegliamo, 2. mi diverto, 3. si alzano, 4. si svegliano, 5. si salutano, 6. si preparano, 7. si lava, 8. si pettina, 9. si incontrano, 10. si divertono, 11. si diverte, 12. si prepara, 13. vi vestite, 14. mi vesto, 15. ci aiutiamo, 16. ci alziamo, 17. ci svegliamo, 18. ci amiamo, 19. ci siamo svegliati, 20. si è alzato, 21. ti sei lavato/a, 22. si è pettinata, 23. si sono odiati/e, 24. si è divertito

Chapter 9

Page 103, Practice 3

A. 1. sto parlando, 2. stai ascoltando, 3 stiamo parlando, 4. sta guidando, 5. sta sentendo, 6. stiamo studiando, 7. state partendo, 8. stai leggendo, 9. sta parlando, 10. sto giocando, 11. stai partendo, 12. stanno tornando

B. 1. stavi andando, 2. stavi ascoltando, 3. stavate parlando, 4. stavo bevendo, 5. stavate vedendo, 6. stavamo giocando, 7. stavate scrivendo, 8. stava leggendo, 9. stavi prendendo, 10. stavo bevendo, 11. stavi partendo, 12. stavo tornando

Page 106, Practice 6

I want to go	I must study	I can bring
we wanted to leave	we had to arrive	we could hear
he/she will want to bring	he/she will have to run	he/she will be able to buy
they wanted to listen	they had to do	they could tell
they wanted to come	they had to go	they could leave

Page 106, Practice 7

voglio pensare	devo andare	posso cantare
volevi scrivere	dovevi vedere	potevi leggere
vorremmo venire	dovremmo comprare	potremmo vendere
hanno voluto giocare	hanno dovuto chiudere	avrebbero potuto pulire

Page 107, Practice 8

1. when was the bill paid?, 2. by whom was the Divine Comedy written? 3. America was discovered in 1492, 4. the boy was woken up, 5. the house is finished

Page 107, Practice 9

1. l'inglese è studiato da molti, 2. la partita è stata giocata sotto la pioggia, 3. quando è stato trovato il cane? 4. la casa è pulita da Paolo, 5. la macchina è stata venduta in fretta

Page 109, Practice 10

Present
1. disdico, 2. rifai, 3. fraintendete, 4. intervengono, 5. tolgo, 6. rifa, 7. suppongono, 8. ottiene, 9. interdicono, 10. rivediamo

Future
1. rifarò, 2. contenderanno, 3. supporrà, 4. prevedremo, 5. rifarete, 6. opporremo, 7. otterranno, 8. predirò, 9. contraddirà, 10. interverranno

Passato Remoto
1. addivennero, 2. previde, 3. soddisfecero, 4. predicemmo, 5. tolsi, 6. fraintendeste, 7. propose, 8. contraddissero, 9. prevenisti, 10. contraffecero

Passato Prossimo
1. ho stupefatto, 2. hai opposto, 3. abbiamo disdetto, 4. hanno previsto, 5. ha ottenuto, 6. hai preteso

Page 110, Practice 11

1. predissero, 2. distenderemo, 3. diviene, 4. perverremo, 5. interdirà, 6. supposero, 7. contraffanno, 8. preveniamo, 9. prevedrà, 10. opponi, 11. soddisfaranno, 12. fraintendete, 13. raccolse, 14. contradici, 15. contendemmo, 16. toglierò, 17. stupefaranno, 18. avvide, 19. rifaccio, 20. distendeste, 21. supponiamo, 22. proposi, 23. distogliamo, 24. raccoglie, 25. disdirò, 26. contraffaremo, 27. opponi, 28. diveniste, 29. togliemmo, 30. intervenne

Chapter 10

Page 111, Practice 1

Io:	parlo	vedo	sento	capisco
Tu:	cammini	scrivi	parti	finisci
Lui:	lavora	legge	viene	pulisce
Lei:	cucina	teme	dice	esce
Noi:	insegniamo	vogliamo	scopriamo	offriamo
Voi:	arrivate	vincete	avvenite	riuscite
Loro:	cambiano	perdono	muoiono	salgono

Page 112, Practice 2

cominciavo, parlavi, arrivava, mangiava
perdeva, vinceva, dicevamo, davano
venivamo, capivi, finiva, salivo
parlavo, diventavi, comprava, passavamo
leggevi, eravamo, scrivevate, dovevano
finivamo, dicevate, capivano, finivi
chiudevo, arrivavi, partiva, usciva
cambiavamo, scrivevate, entravano, fuggivi
avevo, dovevi, andavamo, era
potevamo, facevi, usciva, volevano
venivano, diceva, uscivano, finiva
andavo, capivano, finivate, partivi

Page 113, Practice 3

A. 1. I'll eat, 2. you'll (s.) hear, 3. he'll climb, 4. we'll buy, 5. we'll make/do, 6. I'll study, 7. I'll hear, 8. he/she listens, 9. you'll (pl.) leave, 10. you'll (pl.) understand, 11. I'll make/do, 12. you'll (s.) want, 13. you'll (pl.) have to, 14. you'll (pl.) get up, 15. I'll drive, 16. we'll fly, 17. you'll (s.) stop, 18. I'll know, 19. I'll know, 20. we'll arrive, 21. I'll stay, 22. we'll be, 23. you'll (pl.) read

B. 1. andrò, 2. dormirai, 3. mangerà, 4. pulirò, 5. camminerà, 6. chiamerete, 7. ascolterò, 8. cambierai, 9. staremo, 10. entreranno, 11. riderò, 12. potremo, 13. vedrò, 14. andrete, 15. scriveranno, 16. risponderà, 17. dovrò, 18. dimenticherò, 19. pulirà, 20. staranno, 21. farò, 22. chiuderà, 23. berranno

Page 114, Practice 4

	Passato Remoto	Passato Prossimo
Io:	andai	sono andato/a
Tu:	facesti	hai fatto
Lui:	venne	è venuto
Lei:	capì	ha capito
Noi:	vedemmo	abbiamo visto
Voi:	pensaste	avete pensato
Loro:	sentirono	hanno sentito
Io:	stetti	sono stato/a
Tu:	chiedesti	hai chiesto
Lui:	mandò	ha mandato
Lei:	pensò	ha pensato

Page 115, Practice 5

A. 1. I had eaten, 2. we had understood, 3. they had slept, 4. they had left, 5. I had gone, 6. we had been, 7. we had spoken, 8. you (s.) had studied, 9. I had understood, 10. I had closed, 11. you (s.) had heard, 12. we had brought, 13. he had lost, 14. you (pl.) had won, 15. I had telephoned, 16. she had finished, 17. I had been, 18. they had climbed, 19. she had descended, 20. you (pl.) had left, 21. we had been sorry, 22. they had died, 23. I had entered

B. 1. avevo dormito, 2. era entrato, 3. aveva parlato, 4. avevamo capito, 5. avevate fatto, 6. aveva fatto, 7. aveva scritto, 8. eri stato/a, 9. aveva visto, 10. eravamo venuti/e, 11. erano ritornati/e, 12. eravamo andati/e, 13. avevo mangiato, 14. avevi scritto, 15. avevano pulito, 16. avevamo letto, 17. aveva messo, 18. avevamo detto, 19. avevo saputo, 20. aveva visto, 21. avevo voluto, 22. avevate detto, 23. era nata

Page 116, Practice 6

1. vorrei (mi piacerebbe), 2. leggerei, 3. parlereste, 4. ascolterebbe, 5. pulirei, 6. scriverebbero, 7. penseremmo, 8. risponderei, 9. leggeresti, 10. mangerebbe, 11. venderebbe, 12. studieremmo, 13. scierei, 14. viaggerebbero, 15. berreste, 16. studierei, 17. dovrei, 18. potrei, 19. vorresti, 20. penseremmo, 21. chiuderebbero, 22. apriremmo, 23. capirebbe

Page 117, Practice 7

1. avrei voluto (mi sarebbe piaciuto), 2. sarei stato/a, 3. avrebbe parlato, 4. avrei ascoltato, 5. avreste pulito, 6. avrebbero scritto, 7. avrebbero pensato, 8. avrebbe letto, 9. avremmo mangiato, 10. sarebbero arrivati/e, 11. sarei stato/a, 12. saremmo stati/e, 13. avresti bevuto, 14. avrebbe studiato, 15. sarebbe andata, 16. avreste voluto, 17. avrei chiuso, 18. avrebbe aperto, 19. avrebbe pensato, 20. avremmo capito, 21. avrebbero viaggiato, 22. avresti cantato, 23. avrebbero guardato, 24. saremmo venuti/e

Present Subjunctive	Imperfect Subjunctive
1. mangi	mangiassi
2. veda	vedessi
3. parli	parlasse
4. senta	sentisse
5. chiudiamo	chiudessimo
6. capiate	capiste
7. vengano	venissero
8. rispondiamo	rispondessimo
9. scriva	scrivessi
10. impari	imparassi
11. finisca	finisse
12. mangiamo	mangiassimo
13. beviate	beveste
14. sappiano	sapessero
15. telefoni	telefonassi
16. prenda	prendesse
17. stiate	steste
18. stia	stessi
19. dobbiate	doveste
20. capiscano	capissero
21. legga	leggesse
22. mandi	mandassi
23. venda	vendesse

Page 119, Practice 9

1. sia venuto/a	fossi venuto/a
2. abbia parlato	avesse parlato
3. abbiamo ascoltato	avessimo ascoltato
4. abbia fatto	avesse fatto
5. abbiate finito	aveste finito
6. siate andati/e	foste andati/e
7. abbiano chiuso	avessero chiuso
8. abbia aperto	avessi aperto
9. abbia potuto	avessi potuto
10. abbia detto	avesse detto
11. abbiamo finito	avessimo finito
12. abbia capito	avessi capito
13. abbia risposto	avessi risposto
14. abbia visto	avesse visto
15. abbiate parlato	aveste parlato
16. abbia vissuto	avessi vissuto
17. abbia preso	avesse preso
18. abbiano viaggiato	avessero viaggiato
19. abbia ordinato	avessi ordinato
20. abbiate insegnato	aveste insegnato
21. abbia bevuto	avessi bevuto
22. abbia aspettato	avesse aspettato
23. abbia ricevuto	avessi ricevuto

Page 120, Practice 10

	Present	Future	Imperfect	Passato Remoto
Io:	faccio	farò	facevo	feci
Tu:	vai	andrai	andavi	andasti
Lui:	mangia	mangerà	mangiava	mangiò
Lei:	parla	parlerà	parlava	parlò
Noi:	leggiamo	leggeremo	leggevamo	leggemmo
Voi:	bevete	berrete	bevevate	beveste
Loro:	vedono	vedranno	vedevano	videro
Io:	sento	sentirò	sentivo	sentii
Lui:	dà	darà	dava	diede
Voi:	state	starete	stavate	steste
Lei:	capisce	capirà	capiva	capì
Loro:	finiscono	finiranno	finivano	finirono
Io:	rispondo	risponderò	rispondevo	risposi
Lui:	pulisce	pulirà	puliva	pulì
Noi:	arriviamo	arriveremo	arrivavamo	arrivammo
Voi:	salite	salirete	salivate	saliste
Tu:	soffri	soffrirai	soffrivi	soffristi
Lei:	offre	offrirà	offriva	offrì
Io:	imparo	imparerò	imparavo	imparai
Loro:	vede	vedrà	vedeva	vide
Lei:	cade	cadrà	cadeva	cadde
Lui:	muore	morirà	moriva	morì

Page 121, Practice 11

1. ho capito   avevo capito
2. hai visto   avevi visto
3. ha finito   aveva finito
4. ha letto   aveva letto
5. siamo ritornati/e   eravamo ritornati/e
6. avete imparato   avevate imparato
7. hanno cenato   avevano cenato
8. ho pranzato   avevo pranzato
9. ha venduto   aveva venduto
10. ha acceso   aveva acceso
11. avete accettato   avevate accettato
12. hanno spento   avevano spento
13. ho lavato   avevo lavato
14. siamo usciti/e   eravamo usciti/e
15. hai viaggiato   avevi viaggiato
16. è partito   era partito
17. ha guarito   aveva guarito
18. siete arrivati/e   eravate arrivati/e
19. hai ascoltato   avevi ascoltato
20. hanno saltato   avevano saltato
21. ha esaminato   aveva esaminato
22. abbiamo diviso   avevamo diviso
23. ha stirato   aveva stirato

Page 122, Practice 12

1.	parlerei	avrei parlato
2.	arriveresti	saresti arrivato/a
3.	canterebbe	avrebbe cantato
4.	laverebbe	avrebbe lavato
5.	lavorerebbe	avrebbe lavorato
6.	staremmo	saremmo stati/e
7.	andreste	sareste andati/e
8.	viaggerebbero	avrebbero viaggiato
9.	vedrei	avrei visto
10.	potresti	avresti potuto
11.	leggerebbe	avrebbe letto
12.	scriverebbe	avrebbe scritto
13.	correremmo	saremmo corsi/e
14.	rispondereste	avreste risposto
15.	cadrebbero	sarebbero caduti/e
16.	capirei	avrei capito
17.	finiresti	avresti finito
18.	verrebbe	sarebbe venuto/a
19.	sentiremmo	avremmo sentito
20.	offrireste	avreste offerto
21.	pulirebbero	avrebbero pulito

Page 123, Practice 13

	Present	Imperfect	Past	Pluperfect Subjunctive
Io:	vada	andassi	sia andato/a	fossi andato/a
Tu:	ritorni	ritornassi	sia ritornato/a	fossi ritornato/a
Lui:	dia	desse	abbia dato	avesse dato
Lei:	faccia	facesse	abbia fatto	avesse fatto
Noi:	stiamo	stessimo	siamo stati/e	fossimo stati/e
Voi:	beviate	beveste	abbiate bevuto	aveste bevuto
Loro:	vedano	vedessero	abbiano visto	avessero visto
Noi:	fermiamo	fermassimo	abbiamo fermato	avessimo fermato
Lui:	senta	sentisse	abbia sentito	avesse sentito
Lei:	divida	dividesse	abbia diviso	avesse diviso
Lui:	paghi	pagasse	abbia pagato	avesse pagato
Tu:	venda	vendessi	abbia venduto	avessi venduto
Io:	dorma	dormissi	abbia dormito	avessi dormito
Loro:	contino	contassero	abbiano contato	avessero contato
Voi:	diciate	diceste	abbiate detto	aveste detto
Lei:	giochi	giocasse	abbia giocato	avesse giocato
Lui:	salti	saltasse	abbia saltato	avesse saltato
Noi:	guardiamo	guardassimo	abbiamo guardato	avessimo guardato
Tu:	salga	salissi	sia salito/a	fossi salito/a
Voi:	leggiate	leggeste	abbiate letto	aveste letto
Loro:	tirino	tirassero	abbiano tirato	avessero tirato
Noi:	pensiamo	pensassimo	abbiamo pensato	avessimo pensato

Chapter 11

Page 125, Practice 2

1. ho bisogno di scarpe, 2. ho caldo, 3. hai freddo, 4. abbiamo fretta, 5. hanno mal di testa, 6. ho paura, 7. ha sete, 8. aveva sonno, 9. avevano ragione, 10. avevo torto, 11. abbiamo vergogna, 12. ho voglia di mangiare, 13. avevate fame, 14. avevano fretta, 15. avrei sete, 16. avrebbero bisogno di scarpe, 17. avrebbe ragione, 18. avremmo torto, 19. avrei paura, 20. avrebbe intenzione, 21. ho avuto mal di testa, 22. hanno avuto paura, 23. abbiamo avuto paura

Page 128, Practice 4

1. facciamo alla romana, 2. fa attenzione, 3. faccio colazione, 4. facciamo un bagno, 5. hanno fatto una crociera, 6. fa la spesa, 7. ti sei fatto/a male, 8. faccio un favore, 9. fanno una passeggiata, 10. farò fotografie, 11. ha fatto un viaggio, 12. fate una domanda, 13. fa uno spuntino, 14. facciamo in fretta, 15. fa caldo, 16. facciamo un regalo, 17. facciamo una visita, 18. faceva freddo, 19. fa la predica, 20. farà un discorso, 21. fanno quattro chiacchiere, 22. ha fatto brutta figura

Page 133, Practice 10

1. We learn to ski, 2. I start to understand, 3. I forgot to study, 4. I'm thinking of coming, 5. he/she needs to study, 6. he/she thought about you, 7. we'll stay home, 8. they'll return to Rome, 9. I am afraid of everything, 10. they wait to come, 11. I need you, 12. she continues to eat, 13. he/she used to teach driving, 14. you (pl.) hope to see, 15. I realize I'm late, 16. he/she falls in love with everybody, 17. I don't trust him, 18. she lives on love, 19. stop (s.) talking, 20. you count (pl.) on your sister, 21. he/she tried walking, 22. he/she pretends to look in the book, 23. we laugh at him, 24. they give thanks for everything

Page 134, Practice 11

1. vado a ballare, 2. andiamo a studiare, 3. sei stato/a a Roma?, 4. credo nei fantasmi, 5. pensano alle vacanze, 6. proverò a venire, 7. pensiamo di andare, 8. ti insegnerò a nuotare, 9. finisco di lavorare, 10. ha voglia di mangiare cioccolata, 11. comincio a parlare, 12. si ferma a Parigi, 13. cerchiamo di venire, 14. chiamami prima di partire, 15. continui a studiare, 16. hanno promesso di andare, 17. ho promesso di venire, 18. hanno bisogno di pensare, 19. sperate di dormire, 20. hanno voglia di viaggiare, 21. smetti di parlare, 22. fanno attenzione all'insegnante

Verb Charts

Regular Verbs

Verbs Ending in -are

Parlare

Present Indicative
parlo, parli, parla, parliamo,
parlate, parlano

Imperfect
parlavo, parlavi, parlava,
parlavamo, parlavate, parlavano

Future
parlerò, parlerai, parlerà,
parleremo, parlerete, parleranno

Imperative
parla, parliamo, parlate
parli (pol. s.), parlino (pol pl.)

Passato Remoto (Preterite)
parlai, parlasti, parlò,
parlammo, parlaste, parlarono

Passato Prossimo (Present Perfect)
ho parlato, hai parlato, ha parlato,
abbiamo parlato, avete parlato,
hanno parlato

Verbs Ending in -ere

Perdere

perdo, perdi, perde, perdiamo,
perdete, perdono

perdevo, perdevi, perdeva,
perdevamo, perdevate, perdevano

perderò, perderai, perderà,
perderemo, perderete, perderanno

perdi, perdiamo, perdete
perda (pol. s.), perdano (pol. pl.)

perdei, perdesti, perdè,
perdemmo, perdeste, perderono

ho perduto, hai perduto, ha perduto,
abbiamo perduto, avete perduto,
hanno perduto

Parlare

Trapassato Prossimo (Pluperfect)
avevo parlato, avevi parlato,
aveva parlato, avevamo parlato,
avevate parlato, avevano parlato

Present Conditional
parlerei, parleresti, parlerebbe,
parleremmo, parlereste, parlerebbero

Past Conditional
avrei parlato, avresti parlato,
avrebbe parlato, avremmo parlato,
avreste parlato, avrebbero parlato

Present Subjunctive
che io parli, tu parli, lui/lei parli,
noi parliamo, voi parliate,
loro parlino

Imperfect Subjunctive
che io parlassi, tu parlassi,
lui/lei parlasse, noi parlassimo,
voi parlaste, loro parlassero

Past Subjunctive
che io abbia parlato, tu abbia
parlato, lui/lei abbia parlato,
noi abbiamo parlato, voi abbiate
parlato, loro abbiano parlato

Pluperfect Subjunctive
che io avessi parlato, tu avessi
parlato, lui/lei avesse parlato,
noi avessimo parlato, voi aveste
parlato, loro avessero parlato

Perdere

avevo perduto, avevi perduto,
aveva perduto, avevamo perduto,
avevate perduto, avevano perduto

perderei, perderesti, perderebbe,
perderemmo, perdereste, perderebbero

avrei perduto, avresti perduto,
avrebbe perduto, avremmo perduto,
avreste perduto, avrebbero perduto

che io perda, tu perda, lui/lei perda,
noi perdiamo, voi perdiate,
loro perdano

che io perdessi, tu perdessi,
lui/lei perdesse, noi perdessimo,
voi perdeste, loro perdessero

che io abbia perduto, tu abbia
perduto, lui/lei abbia perduto,
noi abbiamo perduto, voi abbiate
perduto, loro abbiano perduto

che io avessi perduto, tu avessi
perduto, lui/lei avesse perduto,
noi avessimo perduto, voi aveste
perduto, loro avessero perduto

Verbs Ending in -ire

Dormire

Present Indicative
dormo, dormi, dorme, dormiamo,
dormite, dormono

Imperfect
dormavo, dormavi, dormava,
dormavamo, dormavate, dormavano

Future
dormirò, dormirai, dormirà,
dormiremo, dormirete, dormiranno

Imperative
dormi, dormiamo, dormite
dorma (pol. s), dormano (pol. pl.)

Passato Remoto (Preterite)
dormii, dormisti, dormì, dormimmo,
dormiste, dormirono

Passato Prossimo (Present Perfect)
ho dormito, hai dormito, ha dormito,
abbiamo dormito, avete dormito,
hanno dormito

Trapassato Prossimo (Pluperfect)
avevo dormito, avevi dormito,
aveva dormito, avevamo dormito,
avevate dormito, avevano dormito

Verbs Ending in -ire (with isc)

Finire

finisco, finisci, finisce, finiamo,
finite, finiscono

finivo, finivi, finiva,
finivamo, finivate, finivano

finirò, finirai, finirà,
finiremo, finirete, finiranno

finisci, finiamo, finite
finisca (pol. s.), finiscano (pol. pl.)

finii, finisti, finì, finimmo,
finiste, finirono

ho finito, hai finito, ha finito,
abbiamo finito, avete finito,
hanno finito

avevo finito, avevi finito,
aveva finito, avevamo finito,
avevate finito, avevano finito

Dormire	**Finire**

Present Conditional

dormirei, dormiresti, dormirebbe,	finirei, finiresti, finirebbe,
dormiremmo, dormireste, dormirebbero	finiremmo, finireste, finirebbero

Past Conditional

avrei dormito, avresti dormito,	avrei finito, avresti finito,
avrebbe dormito, avremmo dormito,	avrebbe finito, avremmo finito,
avreste dormito, avrebbero dormito	avreste finito, avrebbero finito

Present Subjunctive

che io dorma, tu dorma, lui/lei dorma,	che io finisca, tu finisca, lui/lei finisca,
noi dormiamo, voi dormiate,	noi finiamo, voi finiate,
loro dormano	loro finiscano

Imperfect Subjunctive

che io dormissi, tu dormissi,	che io finissi, tu finissi,
lui/lei dormisse, noi dormissimo,	lui/lei finisse, noi finissimo,
voi dormiste, loro dormissero	voi finiste, loro finissero

Past Subjunctive

che io abbia dormito, tu abbia	che io abbia finito, tu abbia
dormito, lui/lei abbia dormito,	finito, lui/lei abbia finito,
noi abbiamo dormito, voi abbiate	noi abbiamo finito, voi abbiate
dormito, loro abbiano dormito	finito, loro abbiano finito

Pluperfect Subjunctive

che io avessi dormito, tu avessi	che io avessi finito, tu avessi
dormito, lui/lei avesse dormito,	finito, lui/lei avesse finito,
noi avessimo dormito, voi aveste	noi avessimo finito, voi aveste
dormito, loro avessero dormito	finito, loro avessero finito

Common Irregular Verbs

Fare	*Dare*
Present Indicative	
faccio, fai, fa, facciamo, fate, fanno	do, dai, dà, diamo, date, danno
Imperfect	
facevo, facevi, faceva, facevamo, facevate, facevano	davo, davi, dava, davamo, davate, davano
Future	
farò, farai, farà, faremo, farete, faranno	darò, darai, darà, daremo, darete, daranno
Imperative	
fà (non fare), facciamo, fate faccia (pol. s.), facciano (pol. pl.)	dà (non dare), diamo, date dia (pol. s.), diano (pol. pl.)
Passato Remoto (Preterite)	
feci, facesti, fece, facemmo, faceste, facero	diedi, desti, diede, demmo, deste, diedero
Passato Prossimo (Present Perfect)	
ho fatto, hai fatto, ha fatto, abbiamo fatto, avete fatto, hanno fatto	ho dato, hai dato, ha dato, abbiamo dato, avete dato, hanno dato
Trapassato Prossimo (Pluperfect)	
avevo fatto, avevi fatto, aveva fatto, avevamo fatto, avevate fatto, avevano fatto	avevo dato, avevi dato, aveva dato, avevamo dato, avevate dato, avevano dato

Fare

Present Conditional
farei, faresti, farebbe,
faremmo, fareste, farebbero

Past Conditional
avrei fatto, avresti fatto,
avrebbe fatto, avremmo fatto,
avreste fatto, avrebbero fatto

Present Subjunctive
che io faccia, tu faccia, lui/lei faccia,
noi facciamo, voi facciate,
loro facciano

Imperfect Subjunctive
che io facessi, tu facessi,
lui/lei facesse, noi facessimo,
voi faceste, loro facessero

Past Subjunctive
che io abbia fatto, tu abbia
fatto, lui/lei abbia fatto,
noi abbiamo fatto, voi abbiate
fatto, loro abbiano fatto

Pluperfect Subjunctive
che io avessi fatto, tu avessi
fatto, lui/lei avesse fatto,
noi avessimo fatto, voi aveste
fatto, loro avessero fatto

Dare

Present Conditional
darei, daresti, darebbe,
daremmo, dareste, darebbero

Past Conditional
avrei dato, avresti dato,
avrebbe dato, avremmo dato,
avreste dato, avrebbero dato

Present Subjunctive
che io dia, tu dia, lui/lei dia,
noi diamo, voi diate,
loro diano

Imperfect Subjunctive
che io dessi, tu dessi,
lui/lei desse, noi dessimo,
voi deste, loro dessero

Past Subjunctive
che io abbia dato, tu abbia
dato, lui/lei abbia dato,
noi abbiamo dato, voi abbiate
dato, loro abbiano dato

Pluperfect Subjunctive
che io avessi dato, tu avessi
dato, lui/lei avesse dato,
noi avessimo dato, voi aveste
dato, loro avessero dato

Vedere	Venire
Present Indicative	
vedo, vedi, vede, vediamo, vedete, vedono	vengo, vieni, viene, veniamo, venite, vengono
Imperfect	
vedevo, vedevi, vedeva, vedevamo, vedevate, vedevano	venivo, venivi, veniva, venivamo, venivate, venivano
Future	
vedrò, vedrai, vedrà, vedremo, vedrete, vedranno	verrò, verrai, verrà, verremo, verrete, verranno
Imperative	
vedi (non vedere), vediamo, vedete veda (pol. s.), vedano (pol. pl.)	vieni (non venire), veniamo, venite venga (pol. s.), vengano (pol. pl.)
Passato Remoto (Preterite)	
vidi, vedesti, vide, vedemmo, vedeste, videro	venni, venisti, venne, venimmo, veniste, vennero
Passato Prossimo (Present Perfect)	
ho visto, hai visto, ha visto, abbiamo visto, avete visto, hanno visto	sono venuto/a, sei venuto/a, lui/lei è venuto/a, noi siamo venuti/e, voi siete venuti/e, loro sono venuti/e
Trapassato Prossimo (Pluperfect)	
avevo visto, avevi visto, aveva visto, avevamo visto, avevate visto, avevano visto	ero venuto/a, eri venuto/a, era venuto/a, eravamo venuti/e, eravate venuti/e, erano venuti/e

Vedere

Present Conditional
vedrei, vedresti, vedrebbe,
vedremmo, vedreste, vedrebbero

Past Conditional
avrei visto, avresti visto,
avrebbe visto, avremmo visto,
avreste visto, avrebbero visto

Present Subjunctive
che io veda, tu veda, lui/lei veda,
noi vediamo, voi vediate,
loro vedano

Imperfect Subjunctive
che io vedessi, tu vedessi,
lui/lei vedesse, noi vedessimo,
voi vedeste, loro vedessero

Past Subjunctive
che io abbia visto, tu abbia
visto, lui/lei abbia visto,
noi abbiamo visto, voi abbiate
visto, loro abbiano visto

Pluperfect Subjunctive
che io avessi visto, tu avessi
visto, lui/lei avesse visto,
noi avessimo visto, voi aveste
visto, loro avessero visto

Venire

Present Conditional
verrei, verresti, verrebbe,
verremmo, verreste, verrebbero

Past Conditional
sarei venuto/a, saresti venuto/a,
sarebbe venuto/a, saremmo venuti/e,
sareste venuti/e, sarebbero venuti/e

Present Subjunctive
che io venga, tu venga, lui/lei venga,
noi veniamo, voi veniate,
loro vengano

Imperfect Subjunctive
che io venissi, tu venissi,
lui/lei venisse, noi venissimo,
voi veniste, loro venissero

Past Subjunctive
che io sia venuto/a, tu sia
venuto/a, lui/lei sia venuto/a,
noi siamo venuti/e, voi siate
venuti/e, loro siano venuti/e

Pluperfect Subjunctive
che io fossi venuto/a, tu fossi venuto/a,
lui/lei fosse venuto/a,
noi fossimo venuti/e, voi foste venuti/e,
loro fossero venuti/e

Index of Verbs

Italian–English

A

abitare to live
accadere to happen
accedere to access
accendere to light
accettare to accept
acconsentire to agree
aderire to adhere
aggiungere to add
aiutare to help
alzarsi to get up
amare to love
andare to go
apparire to appear
appendere to hang
applaudire to applaud
apprendere to learn
aprire to open
arrestare to arrest
arrivare to arrive
ascoltare to listen
aspettare to wait
assentire to consent
assistere to assist
assolvere to absolve
assumere to assume, hire
attendere to attend
attribuire to attribute
avere to have
avvenire to happen
avvertire to announce

B

ballare to dance
bere to drink
benedire to bless
bollire to boil

C

cadere to fall
cambiare to change
camminare to walk
cantare to sing
capire to understand
cenare to have supper
chiedere to ask
chiudere to close
cogliere to gather
colpire to hit
cominciare to start
comprare to buy
comprendere to comprehend
concludere to conclude
condividere to share
confondere to confuse
conoscere to know
consentire to agree
conseguire to result
consistere to consist
contare to count
controllare to control
convertire to convert
convincere to convince
coprire to cover
correggere to correct
correre to run
costruire to build
credere to believe
crescere to grow
cucire to sew
cuocere to cook

D

dare to give
decidere to decide
desiderare to wish
difendere to defend
digerire to digest
dimagrire to lose weight

dimenticare   to forget
dire   to tell, say
dirigere   to direct
discutere   to discuss
distinguere   to distinguish
diventare   to become
divertire   to enjoy
dividere   to divide
domandare   to ask
donare   to donate
dormire   to sleep
dovere   must

E

eleggere   to elect
entrare   to enter
esaminare   to examine
esaurire   to exhaust
esibire   to exhibit
esistere   to exist
esprimere   to express
essere   to be

F

fallire   to fail
fare   to do, make
fermare   to stop
ferire   to wound
finire   to finish
firmare   to sign
fuggire   to escape

G

garantire   to guarantee
gestire   to manage
giocare   to play
girare   to turn
godere   to enjoy
guardare   to look
guarire   to heal
guidare   to drive
gustare   to taste

I

illustrare   to illustrate
imparare   to learn
includere   to include
inghiottire   to swallow
insegnare   to teach
inseguire   to follow, chase
insistere   to insist
interrompere   to interrupt
investire   to invest
ispezionare   to inspect
istruire   to instruct
invadere   to invade
invitare   to invite

L

lasciare   to leave
lavare   to wash
lavorare   to work
leggere   to read
litigare   to quarrel

M

mandare   to send
mangiare   to eat
mentire   to lie
mettere   to put
morire   to die
mostrare   to show
muovere   to move

N

nascere   to be born
nascondere   to hide
nevicare   to snow
notare   to notice
nuotare   to swim

O

offrire   to offer
organizzare   to organize

P

pagare   to pay
parlare   to speak, talk

partire   to leave, depart
pensare   to think
perdere   to lose
perdonare   to forgive
permettere   to allow
piangere   to cry
piantare   to plant
piovere   to rain
porre   to put
portare   to bring
potere   to be able
pranzare   to dine
preferire   to prefer
prendere   to take
pretendere   to pretend
prevenire   to prevent
promettere   to promise
promuovere   to promote
proporre   to propose
proteggere   to protect
provare   to try
provvedere   to provide
pulire   to clean
punire   to punish

R

raccontare   to narrate
raggiungere   to reach
rallentare   to slow down
regalare   to give a gift, donate
restare   to stay
restituire   to return
ricevere   to receive
richiedere   to request
ricordare   to remember
ridere   to laugh
ridurre   to reduce
rimanere   to remain
rimuovere   to remove
riposare   to rest
risolvere   to resolve
rispondere   to answer
ritornare   to return
riunire   to reunite
rompere   to break

S

salire   to climb
saltare   to jump
sapere   to know
scegliere   to choose
scendere   to descend
sciare   to ski
scomparire   to disappear
scoprire   to discover
scrivere   to write
seguire   to follow
sentire   to hear
seppellire   to bury
servire   to serve
soffrire   to suffer
sognare   to dream
sorridere   to smile
sostituire   to substitute
spedire   to send
spegnere   to turn off
spendere   to spend
sperare   to hope
spiegare   to explain
spingere   to push
stabilire   to establish
stare   to stay
stirare   to iron
studiare   to study
succedere   to happen
suggerire   to suggest
suonare   to play
svegliare   to wake up
svenire   to faint

T

tagliare   to cut
telefonare   to telephone
temere   to fear
tenere   to keep
togliere   to remove
tornare   to return
tradire   to betray
tradurre   to translate
trasferire   to transfer
trasmettere   to broadcast
trovare   to find

U

ubbidire   to obey
udire   to hear
unire   to unite
urlare   to scream
uscire   to go out

V

valere   to be worth
vedere   to see

vendere   to sell
venire   to come
vestire   to dress
viaggiare   to travel
vincere   to win
visitare   to visit
vivere   to live
volare   to fly
volere   to want
votare   to vote

Index of Verbs

English–Italian

A

absolve **assolvere**
accept **accettare**
access **accedere**
add **aggiungere**
adhere **aderire**
agree **acconsentire**
answer **rispondere**
appear **apparire**
applaud **applaudire**
arrest **arrestare**
arrive **arrivare**
ask **chiedere**
assist **assistere**
assume **assumere**
attend **attendere**
attribute **attribuire**

B

be **essere**
be born **nascere**
become **diventare, divenire**
believe **credere**
betray **tradire**
bless **benedire**
blow up **gonfiare**
boil **bollire**
break **rompere**
bring **portare**
build **costruire**
bury **seppellire**
buy **comprare**

C

call **chiamare**
can **potere**
cancel **cancellare**
change **cambiare**
choose **scegliere**

clean **pulire**
climb **salire**
close **chiudere**
come **venire**
complete **completare**
comprehend **comprendere**
conclude **concludere**
confuse **confondere**
consent **consentire**
control **controllare**
convert **convertire**
convince **convincere**
cook **cuocere**
correct **correggere**
count **contare**
cover **coprire**
cry **piangere**
cut **tagliare**

D

dance **ballare**
decide **decidere**
defend **difendere**
define **definire**
depart **partire**
descend **scendere**
die **morire**
digest **digerire**
dine **cenare**
direct **dirigere**
disappear **sparire**
discover **scoprire**
discuss **discutere**
distinguish **distinguere**
divide **dividere**
do **fare**
donate **donare**
dream **sognare**
dress **vestire**
drink **bere**

E

eat **mangiare**
elect **eleggere**
enjoy **godere**
enter **entrare**
escape **fuggire**
establish **stabilire**
examine **esaminare**
exhaust **esaurire**
exhibit **esibire**
exist **esistere**
expire **scadere**
explain **spiegare**
express **esprimere**

F

fail **fallire**
fall **cadere**
fear **temere**
feed **nutrire**
find **trovare**
finish **finire**
flee **scappare**
fly **volare**
follow **seguire**
forget **dimenticare**
forgive **perdonare**

G

gather **raccogliere**
get up **alzarsi**
give up **arrendersi**
give **dare**
give a gift **regalare**
go **andare**
go crazy **impazzire**
go out **uscire**
grow **crescere**
guarantee **garantire**

H

hang **appendere**
happen **accadere**
have **avere**
heal **guarire**
hear **sentire, udire**
help **aiutare**
hide **nascondere**
hope **sperare**

I

illustrate **illustrare**
include **includere**
insert **inserire**
insist **insistere**
inspect **ispezionare**
install **installare**
instruct **istruire**
interrupt **interrompere**
invite **invitare**

J

jump **saltare**

K

keep **tenere**
know (something) **sapere**
know (somebody) **conoscere**

L

laugh **ridere**
learn **imparare**
leave **lasciare, partire**
lie **mentire**
listen **ascoltare**
live **vivere**
look **guardare**
lose **perdere**
lose weight **dimagrire**
love **amare**

M

make **fare**
move **muovere**
must **dovere**

N

notify **avvertire**

O

obey **obbedire**
offer **offrire**
organize **organizzare**

P

paint **dipingere**
pay **pagare**
permit **permettere**
plant **piantare**
play **giocare, suonare**
prefer **preferire**
pretend **pretendere**
prevent **prevenire**
proceed **procedere**
promise **promettere**
propose **proporre**
protect **proteggere**
provide **provvedere**
punish **punire**
put **mettere**

R

rain **piovere**
reach **raggiungere**
read **leggere**
receive **ricevere**
reduce **ridurre**
remain **rimanere**
remember **ricordare**
remove **spostare**
request **richiedere**
resolve **risolvere**
rest **riposare**
result **conseguire**
return **ritornare, tornare**
reunite **riunire**
run **correre**

S

say **dire**
scream **urlare**
see **vedere**

sell **vendere**
send **mandare**
serve **servire**
sew **cucire**
share **condividere**
show **mostrare**
sign **firmare**
sing **cantare**
ski **sciare**
sleep **dormire**
slow down **rallentare**
smile **sorridere**
snow **nevicare**
speak **parlare**
spend **spendere**
start **cominciare**
stay **stare**
stop **fermare**
study **studiare**
substitute **sostituire**
succeed **avere successo**
suffer **soffrire**
swallow **inghiottire**
swim **nuotare**

T

take **prendere**
take off **partire**
taste **assaggiare, gustare**
teach **insegnare**
tell **dire**
think **pensare**
transfer **trasferire**
translate **tradurre**
transmit **trasmettere**
travel **viaggiare**
try **provare**
turn **girare**
turn off **spegnere**

U

understand **capire**
unite **unire**

V

visit **visitare**

vote **votare**

W

wait **aspettare**

walk **camminare**

wash **lavare**

wish **desiderare**

work **lavorare**

write **scrivere**

FOREIGN LANGUAGE BOOKS AND MATERIALS

Spanish
Vox Spanish and English Dictionaries
Cervantes-Walls Spanish and English Dictionary
NTC's Dictionary of Spanish False Cognates
NTC's Dictionary of Common Mistakes in Spanish
Complete Handbook of Spanish Verbs
Guide to Spanish Suffixes
Nice 'n Easy Spanish Grammar
Spanish Verbs and Essentials of Grammar
Side by Side Spanish and English Grammar
Spanish Verb Drills
Getting Started in Spanish
Guide to Spanish Idioms
Guide to Correspondence in Spanish
Diccionario Básico Norteamericano
Diccionario del Español Chicano
Basic Spanish Conversation
Stories from Mexico/Historias de México
Stories from Latin America/Historias de Latinoamérica
Let's Learn Spanish Picture Dictionary
My First Spanish and English Dictionary
Spanish Picture Dictionary
Welcome to Spain
Destination Spain
Spanish for Beginners
Spanish à la Cartoon
101 Spanish Idioms
El alfabeto
Let's Sing and Learn in Spanish
Let's Learn Spanish Coloring Book
Let's Learn Spanish Coloring Book-Audiocassette Package
My World in Spanish Coloring Book
Easy Spanish Word Games and Puzzles
Easy Spanish Crossword Puzzles
Easy Spanish Vocabulary Puzzles
Easy Spanish Word Power Games
How to Pronounce Spanish Correctly
Spanish by Association

French
NTC's New College French and English Dictionary
NTC's Dictionary of Faux Amis
NTC's Dictionary of French Faux Pas
NTC's Dictionary of Canadian French
French Verbs and Essentials of Grammar
French Verb Drills
Side by Side French and English Grammar
French Reference Grammar
Real French
Getting Started in French
Guide to French Idioms
Guide to Correspondence in French
Nice 'n Easy French Grammar
French à la Cartoon
French for Beginners
Let's Learn French Picture Dictionary
French Picture Dictionary
Welcome to France
The French-Speaking World
L'alphabet
The French Culture Coloring Book
Let's Learn French Coloring Book
Let's Learn French Coloring Book-Audiocassette Package
My World in French Coloring Book
Easy French Crossword Puzzles
Easy French Vocabulary Games
Easy French Grammar Puzzles
Easy French Word Games

Easy French Culture Games
How to Pronounce French Correctly
L'Express: Ainsi va la France
L'Express: Aujourd'hui la France
Au courant: Expressions for Communicating in Everyday French
French by Association

Audio and Video Language Programs
Just Listen 'n Learn: Spanish, French, Italian, German, Greek, Arabic, Russian, and Japanese
Just Listen 'n Learn PLUS: Spanish, French, and German
Conversational...in 7 Days: Spanish, French, German, Italian, Japanese, Russian, Greek, Portuguese, Arabic, Thai
Practice & Improve Your...Spanish, French, German, and Italian
Practice & Improve Your...Spanish, French, German, and Italian PLUS
Improve Your...Spanish, French, German, and Italian: The P&I Method
Nissan's Business Japanese and Business Japanese PLUS
VideoPassport French and Spanish
Listen & Learn 101 Japanese Idioms

German
Schöffler-Weis German and English Dictionary
Klett German and English Dictionary
Das Max and Moritz Buch
NTC's Dictionary of German False Cognates
Getting Started in German
German Verbs and Essentials of Grammar
Guide to German Idioms
Guide to Correspondence in German
Streetwise German
Nice 'n easy German Grammar
German à la Cartoon
Let's Learn German Picture Dictionary
German Picture Dictionary
German for Beginners
German Verb Drills
Easy German Crossword Puzzles
Easy German Word Games and Puzzles
Let's Learn German Coloring Book
Let's Learn German Coloring Book-Audiocassette Package
My World in German Coloring Book
How to Pronounce German Correctly
Der Spiegel: Aktuelle Themen in der Bundesrepublik Deutschland
German by Association

Italian
Zanichelli Super-Mini Italian and Dictionary
Zanichelli New College Italian and English Dictionary
Basic Italian Conversation
Getting Started in Italian
Complete Handbook of Italian Verbs
Italian Verbs and Essentials of Grammar
Italian Verb Drills
Let's Learn Italian Picture Dictionary
My World in Italian Coloring Book
Let's Learn Italian Coloring Book
Let's Learn Italian Coloring Book-Audiocassette Package
How to Pronounce Italian Correctly
Italian by Association

Greek and Latin
NTC's New College Greek and English Dictionary
Essentials of Latin Grammar

Russian
NTC's Compact Russian and English Dictionary
Complete Handbook of Russian Verbs
Basic Structure Practice in Russian
Easy Russian Phrasebook and Dictionary
Essentials of Russian Grammar
Everyday Conversations in Russian
Business Russian
Roots of the Russian Language
Inspector General
Reading and Translating Contemporary Russian
First Reader in Russian
Stories from Today's Russia
How to Pronounce Russian Correctly

Polish
The Wiedza Powszechna Compact Polish and English Dictionary

Hebrew
Everyday Hebrew

Japanese
NTC's New Japanese and English Character Dictionary
101 Japanese Idioms
Japanese in Plain English
Japanese Verbs and Essentials of Grammar
Everyday Japanese
Japanese for Children
Konnichi wa Japan
Japanese for the Travel Industry
Japan Today!
Easy Japanese
Easy Hiragana
Easy Katakana
Easy Kana Workbook
How to Pronounce Japanese Correctly
NTC's Dictionary of Japan's Cultural Code Words

Korean
Korean in Plain English

Chinese
Easy Chinese Phrasebook and Dictionary
Basic Chinese Vocabulary
NTC's Dictionary of China's Cultural Code Words

Indonesia
Everyday Indonesia

Malay
Everyday Malay

Swedish
Essentials of Swedish Grammar

Ticket to...Series
France, Germany, Spain, Italy (Guidebook and Audiocassette)

"Just Enough" Phrase Books
Chinese, Dutch, French, German, Greek, Hebrew, Hungarian, Italian, Japanese, Portuguese, Russian, Scandinavian, Serbo-Croat, Spanish, Turkish
Business French, Business German, Business Spanish

BBC Phrase Books
Spanish, French, German, Italian, Greek, Portuguese, Turkish, Arabic

PASSPORT BOOKS
a division of *NTC Publishing Group*
Lincolnwood, Illinois USA